# FINDING JOY WHEN LIFE GETS TOUGH

# FINDING JOY WHEN LIFE GETS TOUGH

VERA HARDIMAN

Bekker Media

# Contents

PART FIVE
TOWARDS A THEOLOGY OF SUFFERING

I dedicate this book to my outstanding husband and sons, their beautiful wives, and my gorgeous grandchildren.
I treasure you all beyond words.

# Acknowledgements

I thank the Lord for asking me to put my thoughts on paper and for inspiring me. Thank you, dearest Holy Spirit for being my ever-present Comforter, Advocate and Guide.

My husband, Ben, has been a wonderful support not only throughout the process of writing this book, but throughout the past almost forty years.

Thank you also to my friend and neighbour Lyn, who has kindly let me glimpse into her amazing life and share her experience and beliefs.

**Through all the years.**
**In all their suffering, He also suffered.**
**And he personally rescued them.**
**In His love and mercy, He redeemed them.**
**He lifted them up and carried them.**
Isaiah 63: 9 (New Living Translation)

# Foreword

I have known Vera for over 20 years. We met at Yarra Valley Vineyard Church, Victoria, Australia, where so many people gathered from all different denominations in search of that radical middle expression of Christianity. We all had one desire - to worship the Lord in intimacy, and we were hungry for the Holy Spirit's presence. Wonderful healings took place in those early years, especially inner healing.

Vera has always been a prayer warrior and has a listening ear to hear what the Holy Spirit is saying. Her faith has been strong through adversity and sickness, and this book is full of wisdom and insight that will encourage your heart when life turns corners that are painful and arduous.

As she shares her journey with you, may the Holy Spirit fill your mind and heart with His healing presence.

**Vicky Merritt, Home Group Leader and Church Planter.**

# Introduction

Let's face it, we all look at life through our own filters. Some of us gaze at life through rose-coloured glasses, or so the saying goes.

If we dared to remove those tinted lenses for a moment, we would suddenly become aware of the stark reality that there is pain all around us.

We do not like it. We hate to acknowledge it, but it is right there in the middle of our lives and in people all around us.

There is the pain of separation and divorce. There is the pain of broken friendships. There is the unhealed illness in our bodies. There is the degeneration of growing older and the loneliness of many.

Pain takes many shapes and is never pleasant, unless you tend towards masochism. Masochism is not my field of interest. I will most gladly leave the task of writing that particular book to someone else.

I am having enough fun (I am being facetious, here) battling with a neurodegenerative disease called Parkinson's. 'Parkinson'. It sounds incredibly old fashioned, like the name of a butler.

Yet, Mr Parkinson is no servant. He is more of a burglar. He continues to rob me of the simplest freedoms: the freedom to move when and where I want and the freedom to talk whenever I wish.

Six years before I was diagnosed, my brother and sister-in-law perished in their home in Marysville, Victoria on Black Saturday, 2009. It was a horrific bushfire that killed hundreds of people in my State of Victoria, Australia. Thousands lost their homes. It took me several years of intense grief before I enjoyed the freedom to be happy again.

While it is great that the church puts a strong emphasis on healing, we rather desperately need a theology of suffering. How should we manage with the suffering we face? Even if we are eventually healed, what do we do in the meantime? Do we just enter some waiting room, where we linger aimlessly until we find the right demon to evict and /or the right sin to repent of so that the way can be cleared for healing to come?

Is there meaning and purpose to our suffering? How does the Lord help us through it?

This world does not provide any person with an entirely smooth ride. When the road gets bumpy, we should not be surprised, but we do need help to cope.

During my private prayer time, sometime in the month of September 2023, I believe the Lord prompted me to write this book. I have been very reliant on the Lord for clarity and revelation during the entire process.

This book is not an attempt to pull together a complete theology of suffering. I have just gathered some thoughts to get the ball rolling, so to speak.

In John 16: 33, the beloved Apostle quotes Jesus saying, **"In this world you will have trouble. Be of great cheer, for I have overcome the world."** (NIV)

At no point does the Lord promise us a completely pain free world.

How do we cope when trouble comes?

In writing this book, I am letting you into my private world, opening the window on my own daily struggles and thoughts.

Where does my comfort come from? Am I still hopeful? Where do I find things to laugh about?

Each of us is on a unique journey. Your pain could well be quite different from mine. I believe that the Lord gives us comfort and glimpses of extraordinary joy, on this side of eternity.

I am writing this book for anyone who is faced with suffering, whether it be a debilitating disease, grief, or loneliness. It would also help those who are supporting others who are suffering.

As we are nearing the 'End of this Age', an increase in lawlessness and suffering has been prophesied. At the same time, we have been promised greater authority and ability to tap into the Lord's immense power resources. At any rate, it appears that there is turbulence ahead.

This has not been an easy book to write. Suffering is by no means a straightforward topic.

Be blessed as you read it. Hopefully, it will bring you comfort, insight and a goodly (as my mother-in-law would say) dollop of good cheer.

As believers travelling through our earthly life, we have chosen a rickety, uncomfortable path. There is tremendous joy to be found there, and sadness too.

As you read this book, dear reader, you will find an interlude every few pages; it may be a piece of scripture to read, or an activation. This is to give you some respite from the topic.

As fellow sufferers with Christ, we all need to engage in some self-care. Jesus withdrew from the crowds to spend time with the Father. We need to learn from His example.

Think of the interlude as a micro sabbath, a time to rest and be restored.

This book can also be used as a 40-day devotional. There is a prayer at the end of each of the forty chapters and there are recommended Scripture readings throughout.

Come on then, let us get started. Let me welcome you into my living room. Do make yourself comfortable and let me confide in you.

# A Prayer for the Reader

*O Holy One of Israel, I ask that you surround each and every reader of this book with a very tangible sense of your strengthening presence. Comfort and protect each one and guide them into your glorious truth.*
*I pray these things in the mighty name of the King of Kings and the Lord of Lords, the name that is above all names, Jesus Christ of Nazareth.*

# PART ONE

# TROUBLE IN THIS WORLD

# I

# A Bit About Myself

*Don't be afraid, for I am with you; don't be discouraged, for I am your God. I will strengthen you and help you. I will hold you up with my victorious right hand.*

Isaiah 41 :10 (NLT)[1]

I remember it clearly.

On 29 January 2015, I found myself in a specialist's surgery, nervously perched on the edge of my seat. On the other side of the desk sat the lady I would later nickname 'My Russian spy'.

This glamorous neurologist, who could have easily been cast in a James Bond movie, was about to deliver her verdict. Tears were welling up in her eyes.

I had been referred to her because of a cluster of strange symptoms. I had turned sixty the previous April and had begun to feel strangely unwell soon after my birthday. The symptoms were nebulous. I just knew something was wrong. Treatment with an osteopath and an ultrasound to check for ovarian cancer had failed to provide answers.

When my GP saw me limping, she finally suggested an MRI, after which she promptly referred me to this neurologist. "I am sorry to have to tell you that you have Parkinson's," was her verdict. "The good news is that it is the classic, most treatable form of Parkinson's."

Surely those words were not directed at me. I did not bother looking behind me. Apart from my husband, Ben, sitting patiently beside me, there was no one else in the office.

At that point in the conversation, I felt as if I had crawled into a giant fishbowl and the words I was hearing were weirdly echoing outside.

I was in shock, and I was hoping that my dear husband, Ben, was listening carefully. I was drifting in and out of the room, mentally, as I tried to grasp what this news was going to mean for me.

I was still working fulltime as a lawyer, managing a community legal centre, with a staff of fifteen.

And I was, and still am, a charismatic Christian believer who believed in miraculous healing.

I knew that Michael J. Fox had been diagnosed with Parkinson's.

Such was my train of thought as I grappled with the news.

After Ben drove me home, I climbed into bed, pulled the doona over my head, and cried. I lay in silence. I pondered. I tried to avoid 'catastrophic' thinking, being that destructive thought pattern where you foolishly allow yourself to imagine all the possible, horrific scenarios that could happen in your life.

My mother had been very empathetic towards my late sister-in-law, Marlene. Marlene's mother had Parkinson's and she would always speak about her visits to her mother's residential care facility in hushed and horrified tones.

All I really knew about Parkinson's was that the disease was neuro-degenerative, and Michael J. Fox suffered from it.

# Prayer

Whatever you are facing, whether it be your diagnosis or that of a loved one, or some other type of suffering, you need the Lord's close presence.

*My dear Lord, I put myself into your capable hands. Come Lord Jesus, come.*

# 2

# Growing Up

**You know my thoughts even when I am far away.**
**You know what I am going to say even before I say it.**
Psalm 139:2 and verse 4 (NLT)

During that first week after my diagnosis, I could not help but wonder what my life would look like now.

Let me tell you who I was before my diagnosis.

I had been through a lot, and I mean a lot, of inner healing. I had felt misunderstood, unpopular, inferior, and painfully shy most of my life.

My parents, two brothers and I migrated from Germany to Australia soon after my only surviving grandparent, my Oma, died in June of 1960, I was six years old. Lo and behold, two years after arriving in Australia, my parents had another baby, my younger brother, Edgar.

I had a lonely childhood growing up in a small town in the Dandenong Ranges outside Melbourne, Australia. My parents never wanted us to bring our school friends to our home. I guess they did not think our home was good enough. A number of my migrant friends grew up in isolated households for one reason or another.

I had numerous imaginary friends, well beyond the years when you are supposed to have them. When I was thirteen, I am embarrassed to admit, I even had an imaginary boarding school organised in my home.

After secondary school, I was off to Melbourne University to study French and German Language and Literature. I was hoping to find the meaning of life. It was naive of me. I was ill-prepared for life at this stage, being only seventeen when I moved into a flat near the university with my two older brothers. I felt very grown up indeed.

Together with my new boyfriend, whom I met on the first day of Orientation Week, we used to stay up into the wee small hours, having many stimulating discussions about the meaning of life, existentialism and more. Oh, we felt we knew it all! We drank Coke in huge quantities, wolfed down Tim Tam chocolate biscuits, explored the late nightlife of Carlton, often dashing out for a souvlaki at the "Twins", a late-night takeaway that stayed open until about 2am. Actual twins helped manage the shop. I gather it was a family business. They also sold fish and chips and hamburgers. It was an incredibly special time in my life, living in the city, refreshingly different from the rural Dandenong Ranges

By the August of that year, I had married my boyfriend. I was far too emotionally immature, but I felt this would be the road to my emancipation from my parents. It was a recipe for disaster.

I soon realised that university was not going to help me in my search for meaning either. I could not believe that people around me could just continue living without knowing the meaning of life.

My husband and I dropped out of university, got jobs, moved into a share house so that I could experience the proverbial Carlton 70's share house, and then trotted off to Europe like many other Melburnians in search of adventure. You may not be able to imagine it now, but in 1976 Melbourne was still a very dull backwater.

With my husband earning danger money from working in a meat freezer, we had soon saved up enough money for one-way airfares to Europe and extra spending money. I had put all my hope in this trip. It was going to provide answers, or so I desperately hoped.

After living and working in Germany for eighteen months, we were both ready to tackle the study of law back in Australia. We got our degrees at the University of Tasmania by 1983 and had a beautiful baby boy by 1981.

# Interlude

I will be like a shepherd looking for his scattered flock. I will find my sheep and rescue them from all the places where they were scattered on that dark and cloudy day.
Ezekiel 34: 12 (NLT)

# 3

## Turmoil Of Youth

Life certainly appeared dark during those years. I had everything I wanted – a husband, a baby, a house, income, friends, but I was still unsatisfied. The truth seemed to be concealed from me.

A dear nun, my grade five teacher, Sister Mary Vincent Joseph, had introduced me to Jesus when I was ten years old. Unfortunately, she told me, and my mother confirmed this, that Jesus would not talk to me when I prayed. That meant that I closed my ears to any possible communication with my Lord, and my conversations with Jesus were very one way and not terribly satisfying.

By the time I was a teenager, I was beginning to find the practice of Catholicism tiring and unhelpful. I gave it up when I was nineteen.

I had fallen in love and married at the very early age of eighteen in an attempt to escape my feelings of abandonment and loneliness.

When I was fully qualified, I discovered that I was very fearful of clients and terrified of making a mistake as a lawyer. I did not feel I belonged in the legal scene.

Germans generally do not do small talk. I was inept at making light conversation. I did not learn to relate on that superficial level, but business chatter relied on the ability to connect over the trivial things, like sport and fashion. I simply did not fit in this way. Maybe if I had been a believer at that stage of my life, I would have found a solution.

Predictably, this led to our marriage breaking down, at which time I had a cute little four-year-old son.

Not long after that I repartnered and had a gorgeous second son. We lived in a Federation timber home in a lovely leafy Melbourne suburb. I married my partner Ben, who trained as a computer expert soon after the wedding.

I was reasonably content, although deep down I was still feeling frighteningly inadequate.

As a child I had a rather unsatisfactory relationship with Jesus. I still remember looking out of my Grade five classroom window and making a promise to the Lord. I promised Him that if He showed me that He existed, by some miraculous sign, that I would then totally give myself to Him.

Now that my firstborn was attending school, I made friends with some of the other mothers. One of the mothers, Sue, had become a Christian. This intrigued me since I had always thought that Christians were rather lacking in brainpower! This lady was well educated and smart.

Anyway, what I was really looking for at the time was an opportunity to join a discussion group, as domestic life left me bored and hungry for some intellectual stimulation. Sue talked about discussions they had had in a small group at church. However, she made it quite clear that these small groups were only open to Christians.

I confided in Sue that I wanted to believe, but simply could not. She recommended that I read the Bible and ask God to reveal Himself to me.

Meanwhile, a friend of my husband, Jim, who was into seances, told us there was a dark-haired ghost in the back room of our home. This was more than a little alarming.

When I mentioned our spiritual boarder to Sue, she did not really comment, except to say that her husband sometimes prayed through houses to get rid of evil spirits.

I filed that piece of information away in my mental filing system for later.

When Sue was eventually baptised, she invited me to the ceremonial dunking.

I sensed there was something different in her church. It was hard to describe what it was. I remember commenting that it felt as if there were bubbles of champagne floating through the air. She explained that I was probably discerning the Holy Spirit.

After the service, I went home and sat myself down in our lounge room to watch something on television. At that point I sensed a dark and disturbing presence standing behind me.

# Prayer

*Lord, I confess that the future scares me. I am wrapping my fear into a parcel. I am covering it up with brown paper and tying string around the outside. Now I am handing all of my fear to you, O Lord. In exchange, I receive your love.*
*Thank you, glorious King.*

# 4

## Finding The Lord

**For our struggle is not against flesh and blood but against the
rulers, against the authorities, against the powers of this dark world
and against the spiritual forces of evil in the heavenly realms.**
Ephesians 6:12 (NIV)

I called Sue and she said she would have people over to my house the
next day who would pray through the house to get rid of the ghost.

The movie *Ghostbusters* had been a favourite of mine at the time,
and here I was experiencing my very own ghostbusters scenario. It was
somehow terrifying and thrilling at the very same time.

The men prayed through the house in my absence. When I returned,
they said that I now had to become a Christian. I replied that I would
have to believe in Jesus before I followed Him. I still had not been able
to believe in Jesus.

They recommended that I ask the Holy Spirit into the house. Otherwise, the demons would return sevenfold.

So, I sat down with my elder son, and we did just that.

I feel there needs to be a drum roll at this point in my story. Drum
roll! Drum roll!

The next morning, I woke at 6am. To my surprise and absolute delight, there was the sublime presence of none other than the Living God in my bedroom. I knew it had to be God, because I felt a joy, and peace and a sense of wholeness in the room, which I was able to discern but had never experienced before.

God spoke to me by dropping words into my brain. That is the only way I can describe it. He said that He did exist and that the stories about His Son were true.

I then took the opportunity to ask God the big question, "What is the meaning of life?"

He answered me by showing me some sad faces in the bedroom window, like in a trance, and He said,

"To bring that feeling of peace, wholeness and joy that you are experiencing now to other people."

The next question I asked was, "Why me?"

I felt I had not done anything to deserve a meeting like this with the living God.

I felt prompted to open the book of Ephesians, which was on the bedside table next to me, and I was directed to the following scripture:

**Salvation is not a reward for the good things you have done, so none of us can boast about it.**
Ephesians 2:9 (NLT)

Before too long I was at Sue's house, giving my heart to the Lord.

About a year later, my husband, Ben, also became a Christian. He had become really curious about what had happened to me. He did a "Christianity Explained"[2] course and became a Christian that way.

What followed were seventeen years of deep inner healing prayer. The healing in my soul empowered me to practice law, including dealing with clients, managing staff, having the wisdom to give accurate and helpful advice and to believe God for miracles. Miraculous outcomes for my clients became my bread and butter, and my faith skyrocketed.

# Prayer

*Lord, may my faith skyrocket at this time.*
*Strengthen and fill me with your Holy Spirit power.*
*I adore you Precious One.*

# 5

## The Daily Struggle

I will give you a glimpse into how I spend my days with the disease, which I refuse to call 'my disease'. I do not own it. I am keen to discard it.

Most days, I experience a great deal of stiffness throughout my body, including my lips. Spasms affect my legs and sometimes my arms and face.

Even now, my discomfort free window, (I call it my 'bliss spot') is about six hours per day.

Throughout the course of each day, starting at about 5am, at three hourly intervals, I take five Madopar pills[3]. I have to take a pill every three hours so that I do not turn into a 'statue' - my body becomes completely stiff without my levodopa /carbidopa. Even my lips are very stiff, so that I have great trouble speaking coherently.

For the first hour after taking my pill in the morning, I have debilitating spasms in my legs. That is because my dopamine levels are too high. In time, the dopamine levels drop, and my body loosens up a little.

Then I have an hour when I function well. As it gets closer to the time when I need to take the second pill, after about two hours, I again stiffen up and have spasms in my legs. That pattern continues throughout most days. Some days are much better and others worse. The more relaxed I am, the better. Unfortunately, a substantial number of things cause me stress, for example, attending a Zoom meeting, having people in my home for a prayer meeting, and any level of confrontation. The spasms take over, even if I have to correct someone quite mildly. Nothing is very predictable about my life.

Overnight, I take a slow-release pill.

In the middle of the night, Ben often pulls me out of bed as and when I need to get up to go to the bathroom. I am very thankful for that. When it gets closer to dawn, I try to fend for myself, as it makes me feel a little more independent. However, by the time I wake up at 4.45am, I am very stiff indeed.

Then I place a Rapid Madipar[4] under my tongue. I am not allowed to take too many of these, as they can cause dyskinesia, which looks like flailing arms, jerky head and so on. That does not make for a very pretty sight and tends to cause people to stare a lot if I am out in public.

A few minutes after taking the Rapid, I can find my way around the kitchen. I then make myself particularly useful by making breakfast. I am glad it works out that way because Ben is by no means a morning person.

If I need to go anywhere, Ben drives me. I am so thankful that he now works from home and most of my activities are close by.

Lyn, my neighbour, drives me to our joint hobbies, like painting and drawing. Ben manages my medication and does the cooking, cleaning, and gardening. He is an absolute star. I am so grateful to have him.

At times I have found it hard to respect myself, as I often feel totally useless. I have to remind myself that I have intrinsic value as a child of God. My value is not related to how 'useful' I am at any given time.

I found it very encouraging to discover that quadriplegic, Joni Eareckson, cannot even manage to brush her own hair. I am not alone.

You and I are treasured possessions of the Lord, whether or not we can brush our own hair or get ourselves out of bed.

This is where our pride comes in. I would love to put on my own seat belt, get myself out of bed, wash myself and be understood when I try to speak. Unfortunately, there have been times when I have had to rely on others to perform these tasks for me. To tell you the truth, it is demeaning.

It is humbling.

## Interlude

The righteous person faces many troubles.
But the Lord comes to the rescue each time.
Psalm 34:19 (NLT)

# Prayer

*Lord, thank you for dying on the cross for me. I gratefully accept the fact that*
*You paid for my sins, and I have been redeemed.*
*I am thrilled that I am now adopted into Your family.*
*If there is any unconfessed sin in my life, please show me*
*so that I can indeed confess it and receive Your merciful forgiveness.*

# 6

# My Path

People with an illness have to walk a fine line in the church today. On the one hand, we are pressing in for healing at every available opportunity. On the other hand, those of us who have not yet been healed need to find our own way to inner peace and encouragement.

That is not always easy.

One thing I have learned is that it is especially important not to identify with the disease.

I am a disciple of Jesus Christ. I do not identify as a PWP[5].

Much as I love the people, I do not wish to spend the bulk of my time with Parkinson's patients. There is more to my life than this ghastly illness. Parkinson's is a defect in the brain - the neurotransmitters are not working properly and are not releasing sufficient dopamine to keep the body moving adequately. This means that the brain and parts of my body are not able to communicate with each other.

Since the late 1960's, medication has been developed which ensures a supply of dopamine to the brain. As I understand it, the medicine works for a limited number of years and then loses its efficacy. The medication does not provide relief to all sufferers of Parkinsonism. Thankfully, the Parkinson's diagnosis I have received is classified as 'classic' and does respond well to treatment.

My paternal Auntie Maria suffered from Parkinsonism in her sixties, at a time before the medication became available. It is unclear whether there is a connection between her illness and mine. I would say that there probably is a connection, as we are remarkably similar in so many ways, looks, personality, habits and more.

As charismatic Christians, we are certainly encouraged to try to find the spiritual cause of our illnesses. I have often been asked to examine what sins I should repent of, or what demon I should evict. This has been good advice and I know of people who have been healed that way.

Having a huge family tree, I am aware of the many and varied unsavoury activities my ancestors have been involved in. Accordingly, I have engaged in quite a bit of representational repentance and have cut generational ties. I have had many demons evicted.

People everywhere have kindly prayed for me. Many have prophesied that I will surely be healed; that may be on the other side of eternity.

I have had so much healing prayer over the years, that I have been 'accidentally' healed of many things. At some point, for example, I went to the audiologist and was informed that my hearing is now perfect (fourteen years ago it had deteriorated somewhat, and I had thought I would need a hearing aid, like my mother).

Another time, a visit to the optometrist revealed that I had to get different glasses because my eyesight had actually improved.

I have also been healed of a frozen shoulder, traumatic grief and labyrinthitis.

There was a time in the community house, about eighteen months ago, when I was suddenly not functioning well. I could not talk or walk, so they put me in a desk chair and wheeled me around. After some healing prayer, I was back walking well again.

One difficulty with suffering is that it does feel lonely at times, especially if there is no one nearby with the same or a similar ailment.

Fear tends to 'hang around' when there is suffering, telling you that things will only get worse. We all need to tell fear to disappear, in no uncertain terms, in the name of the all-powerful Jesus Christ of Nazareth.

I have found the answer is to press into the Lord. He really does turn up to spend time with us, comfort and strengthen us when we persistently make time for him.

Our first reaction to suffering might be that we want to run away. That is a natural response. However, the smart thing to do is to face the suffering with the Lord by our side. That helps us get through.

Trust the Lord, for He is trustworthy. Obey Him and that will open the way to an intimate relationship.[6]

# Prayer

*Dear Lord, more than anything in the whole world,*
*I would like to be close to You.*
*Please help me to hear Your still, small voice,*
*so that I may obey Your every command.*
*Praise be to Your name, Lord Jesus.*

# PART TWO

# OVERCOMING

# 7

## The Tongue And The Will

**The tongue can bring death or life.**
Proverbs 18:21 (NLT)

The tongue is very much like a rudder.

James writes in James 3:4, "**And a small rudder makes a huge ship turn wherever the pilot chooses to go.**" (NLT)

Watch what you say. Listen to your own words.

Carefully craft your sentences, even if it has to be through gritted teeth. Build up and do not tear down.

I find it easy to fall into the habit of saying negative things. An example might be, "That dog never listens." I forget about the power of those words. The words spoken can change the atmosphere, so that yes, that dog is less likely to listen each time that sentence is repeated.

Like our wills, our tongues are powerful tools for both healing and destruction. Just remember the Lord's words in Genesis[7], they brought whole worlds into being. "Let there be light," the Lord said, and there was light.

Speaking negatively is actually quite an easy habit to break. We just need to concentrate. If you find it difficult, record what you say and listen to your words. Are you speaking life or death? Healing or destruction? Improvement or deterioration?

Let us be carriers of God's glory and speak love and light wherever we go.

If someone, for example, says something like, "You will have a hard time doing that," I prefer to say instead, "I am praying that you will have an easy time achieving that."

Do you get the idea?

Practise expressions like, "All will be well."

Bless the people you come across. Bless yourself.

*Please Lord watch over my tongue. I give You permission to remind me, if I speak negatively, to be quiet. Help me to speak life into others and myself.*

Even a tiny engagement of our will can take us a long way. Take, for example, inner vows. When we make inner vows, (usually in moments of weakness) we reap what we sow. I had this experience when I made an inner vow in a moment of pain. I vowed never to get close to anyone ever again.

Then I was 'surprised' to find that I could not make any new friends. Repentance and renunciation did the trick. Once I repented and renounced the vow, I was back to making friends once again.

We have seen in the previous chapter, we looked at how the tongue resembles a rudder. Our will also acts like a rudder.

Like the little, but powerful tongue, a small amount of willpower also takes us a long way.

We are always at liberty to follow our own will or to surrender to God.

We must not remain passive, just waiting for something to happen to us. We need to set our will like a rudder to steer our whole being in the right direction and let us communicate that to the Lord .

This certainly applies to our inner transformation. When I started following the Lord, I became acutely aware of some of my bad attitudes.

I used to have a terrible problem with jealousy. I also felt that I lacked the ability to love others from the heart. In addition to these two qualities, I wanted to be more generous.

I asked the Lord to help me, and I set my will in that direction.

When we bake a cake, we set the oven temperature. Soon enough, the cake batter browns and changes texture.

Imagine with me that we have an imaginary inner dial. When we desire Jesus' character, instead of dialling in the temperature, I believe we can set our imaginary inner dial to 'generosity' and 'love', for example, and we will eventually see these characteristics begin to grow.

As a new believer, I desperately wanted the Lord's character. It took years, but little by little I could see some improvement. Jealousy did not plague me the way it once did. I could rejoice in the success of others, and giving and encouraging became easier to do.

# Interlude

Choose a way to engage your will today. Ask the Lord what He would like to say to you. Is He asking you to change some of your habits or attitudes? Write down what steps you are going to take to do so.

# Prayer

*Heavenly Father, I wish to surrender my will to You this very minute. Please show me what steps I need to take to initiate change in myself. In Your precious name I pray.*

# 8

⧡

# Trauma

Getting back to my diagnosis.

My time of hiding under the doona and indulging in morose self-pity lasted about a week.

Let me explain a bit about Parkinson's disease. It is neurodegenerative, as I pointed out earlier. That means it starts off fairly mild and gets progressively worse, until you become paralysed, unable to move very much at all, unable to talk and feed yourself.

One of the first symptoms I had was dribbling on the right-hand side of my mouth. That appeared soon after my brother and sister-in-law were killed in the bushfires on Black Saturday,[8] 7 February 2009.

They died in their bathroom in Marysville, Victoria Australia. One hundred and thirty-four people in their town died that day.

There are many theories that try to explain the cause of Parkinson's Disease.

Some say it is induced by trauma. The death of my brother could have been the instigator.

Parkinson's is also said to stem from self-hatred. I certainly suffered from that, as my mother made it quite clear to me that I was not the sort of daughter she had wished for herself.

I certainly forgave my mother. I had trauma prayed off my life. I had deliverance and healing prayer. The list goes on.

My driving instructor, who helped me to keep my licence, told me that she had known many people living close to golf courses who had contracted Parkinson's. Our house backed onto a golf course. The culprits were presumed to be the toxic herbicides that golf clubs use.

The cause of the disease no longer preoccupies me. I am too busy trying to live with the disease.

I have accepted that I am not to blame for my illness.

## Interlude

Ask Holy Spirit if you are carrying blame for
something you have not done.

# Prayer

*Help me to align my will with yours, O Lord. I surrender to You, my King.*

# 9

Going After Healing

We are pressed in on every side by our troubles, but we are not
crushed.
We are perplexed but not driven to despair. Through suffering our
bodies continue to share in the death of Jesus so that the life of Jesus
may be seen in our bodies.
2 Corinthians 4:8 (NLT)

As I mentioned earlier, I am a committed charismatic Christian 'Charismatic' to me, means that I believe that God is still actively involved in people's lives, performing healings, deliverance from evil spirits, giving people prophecies (or messages) to pass on to other people.

I completely believe in supernatural healing. I watched my cancer-ridden father come alive under the resurrection power of the Holy Spirit in a healing meeting in 1990. I watched as his skin, which was a deathly grey, become pink and full of life. Filled with joy, he threw his walking stick onto the stage!

My father, Franz Josef Sebald, was seventy-seven at the time. His personality also changed for the better after that, and he reconciled with my eldest brother.

Eventually we were assured of his salvation by a family friend, a nun, who had prayed and sung worship songs with him the day before he died.

After my diagnosis, I felt pressure from many to seek healing wherever it was to be found. The general belief was that I needed to identify the correct demon responsible or find the right way to pray.

Wherever I go, someone kindly offers to pray for healing for me or they prophesy healing.

My hopes have been raised and then dashed countless times.

However, we cannot forgo any healing prayers because we never know which one may well be the effective prayer. The one that is the key that fits the lock and frees me.

I have experienced partial healing and temporary healing. I have given several healing testimonies.

How does Parkinson's disease affect me? At first, before I was medicated, I was hunched over, limping, not able to move my left arm and not able to raise my feet very far off the floor when I walked.

I believe my cognitive function was affected, but I do not exactly remember how. I just know that, when I had prayer with John Mellor,[9] my brain function was healed permanently.

One of my medications, while thankfully lifting my mood, interfered with my ability to control my urges. I tended to overeat and, strange as it may sound, I was addicted to knitting and crochet. I produced one crocheted animal per week.

# *Interlude*

**Fear not; you will no longer live in shame.**
**Do not be afraid; there is no more disgrace for you.**
Isaiah 54:4 (NLT)

If you have fallen into the habit of being too harsh on yourself,
make sure that you forgive yourself and ask the Lord's forgiveness for
being too judgmental of yourself.

# Prayer

*Heavenly Father. Please give me a realistic view of my own identity and help me to encourage myself with healthy thought patterns. Help me to be a decent friend to myself.*

# 10

# Painting And Travel To Israel

In 2016, someone reported me to the local authorities for continuing to drive when I was unwell. My licence was taken away, leaving me terribly angry indeed and in need of an outlet for my fury. As you will no doubt agree, knitting and crochet are very peaceful occupations. It is not easy to knit or crochet aggressively. That is when I started to paint. It was a year and a half after my diagnosis. I could splash paint onto the canvas, draw aggressive creatures using bold and bright colours. These activities calmed me down.

Even then, the Lord provided me with caring and entertaining friends who would transport me to and from work. On the weekends, I took driving lessons and was eventually successfully re-tested for my licence. Thank God I got my licence back, and with renewed confidence too - I was up to date with my road rules and my parking had radically improved with the lessons I had received!

The painting was here to stay. In fact, still on the medication that had removed some of my inhibitions, I would start painting and then enter the 'zone', where I could stay and paint happily for four to five hours at a time.

I managed to take a trip to Israel in 2016 to attend a worship gathering in the Galilee. While at that event, a German physiotherapist treated me with massage and inner healing prayer. I had not sought prayer. She had kindly offered it and I graciously accepted it.

The prayer and treatment improved my condition quite rapidly, giving her the satisfaction of having worked a miracle and giving Ben and me tremendous hope of a better life.

Having given a testimony of my healing at a Messianic service in Tiberias, I ceased my medication regime, and we spent several days in Tel Aviv before catching our flight home.

At that point I relapsed into a hunched over, limping state, even worse than before I had taken any medication.

Sometime after my return to Australia, when all of my efforts could not retrieve the healing I had received in the Galilee, I was hospitalised, as my condition had worsened. The humiliating part was overhearing the male nurse mock me in front of the other nurses in the corridor. "This patient went to Israel, got healing prayer and stopped taking her medication, hehehe." I was a source of great entertainment for them that evening. At least I had been truthful this time. When I first returned, I had not dared tell my GP the truth. As far as she knew, I had simply stopped taking my medication, which rendered me dangerously unstable in her eyes.

The neurologists at the hospital were puzzled and curious. You see, the re-introduced medication was now paralysing me from the neck down. It was a very disconcerting experience. At least I somehow felt safe amongst so many medical professionals.

They explained what I had been told a year or so earlier, that little was known about the brain. Medicating my condition, they assured me, was more of an art than a science. I just had to trust God.

Six weeks later, once I had been discharged from hospital and rehab, my condition[10] had improved. I continued to attend rehab as an out-patient and my condition improved even further.

Then I developed other symptoms, like painful spasms in my legs when my body was low in dopamine. The spasms stayed until I had absorbed the medication. In other words, the spasms occurred just before I was due to take my three hourly medication, as well as after I had taken it. I only had a short discomfort free window of about 1½ hours, five times per day. These were not entirely predictable, as any positive excitement or negative stress also caused these spasms. The spasms were also linked to stiffness in my upper body, which in turn prevented me from talking as it stiffened my lips and neck.

Once, when I was unable to talk, but well able to move my arms, I tried an experiment. I tried talking in tongues in sign language, using weird arm movements which I would probably avoid in company. It was a Holy Spirit inspired sign language that I used in the privacy of my ensuite, to intercede for an important meeting.

Do you know what? Those prayers were answered, not just in the usual way, but with added productivity and enormous amounts of grace. It was the best, most productive meeting.

What I had most predominantly engaged on that occasion, was my will - an incredibly significant rudder indeed.

# Prayer

*Heavenly Father, I know humility is part of vulnerability.*
*Oh, it is hard to give up pride. Empower me,*
*Lord, to fight this battle.*
*I so wish to become like You.*
*Holy Spirit, please come to transform me into the image of Yeshua.*

**Blessed are those who trust in the Lord**
**And have the Lord as their hope and confidence.**
**They are like trees planted along a riverbank.**
**With roots that reach deep into the water.**
**Such trees are not bothered by the heat.**
**Or worried by long months of drought.**
Jeremiah 17:7-8 (NLT)

# 11

# His Unfailing Love

**The Lord's delight is in those who fear him,**
**who put their hope in his unfailing love.**
Psalm 147 :11 (NIV)

I have spent a lot of time sending up "help" prayers over the past eight years. These would be prayers like "Help me be able to talk!" "Help me to get up off this couch", and on it goes.

There was a time when I started thinking that I was becoming a bit of a nuisance to the Lord. I was the nagging lady outside the judge's home in the Gospels.

Let's face it, in the natural, needy people can be annoying at times.

It is not the fault of the needy person. I know there are people who manipulate and feign their neediness. Those people may need a little loving teaching to help open their eyes to the motives behind their own behaviour. Most likely, they need some form of inner healing.

Why doesn't God get a little irritated with our neediness?

The answer is because He is God. He loves us with an everlasting love. He has unlimited resources.

Our irritation is rooted in fear - we are fearful of being drained by the difficult ones. The Lord is never drained. He has infinite love and patience.

He delights in those who hope in His unfailing love.

He does not want us to be independent of Him. Sure, He is also delighted when we go out and pray for the sick, teach the faithful or bring in the lost. However, He always wants to be integrally involved in our work. In fact, without the Holy Spirit we do not have the power to accomplish what the Lord wants and asks of us.

Remember Jesus only did what He saw the Father doing.

It is tricky. The Lord gives us a fully functioning body, soul, and spirit. He equips us and sends us out and then He wants us to rely on Him every step of the way. He wants us to give up control and surrender to Him.

We are inhabitants of an upside-down Kingdom. We say that a lot. Then we are surprised to find it is true.

For the message of the cross "is foolishness to those who are perishing, but to us who are being saved it is the power of God." 1 Corinthians 1:18 (NIV)

The cross, I believe not only refers to the cross of Christ, who died for us, but also to the cross we take up daily, with Jesus as our role model.

At the end of this age, we give up the satisfaction of having achieved success in our lifetime. Then we will throw the crowns, or rewards that we have earned, at the feet of Jesus.

I wonder at the beauty of it all. We are encouraged to each prefer the other. We are taught to regard each other more highly than ourselves.

We, in turn, lift up the Lord in worship and, of course, regard Him to be so much higher than ourselves.

The Lord Jesus only does what He sees the Father doing and calls Him greater than Himself. [11]

Holy Spirit comes and gives to the believers what He has received from Jesus. [12]

The Father glorifies Jesus.

What a glorious picture of community within the Trinity, incorporating us, the believers. A community of deference and love!

I hope I am making sense. I hope you can catch a glimpse of the picture I am trying to paint with words.

For us it is the Kingdom of the Cross, the Kingdom of interdependence, the glory of love and togetherness.

And as we take up the cross of Christ, we become more and more like Him. From death to self, we rise with Jesus, and we go from glory to glory. Hallelujah!

# Interlude

**How do I love thee?**
**Let me count the ways!** [13]

These words of William Shakespeare can be applied to all of us,
as we all abide together with the Lord in everlasting love.
As we pour ourselves out in love for the Lord and each other.
Take a few minutes to just let that sink in.

# Prayer

*I am overawed as I am reminded that the universe is based on love.*
*You are love. You want me to be love.*
*It is too wonderful to comprehend.*
*I love you, Jesus.*

# 12

# Solace From The Lord

Recently, I sought some morning solace in the garden, as my body had stiffened up so much that I could not even manage a short walk with Ben and Alex, our Husky-cross-Staffordshire Terrier.

The garden really relaxes me. I fought my way through the weeds and plonked myself down on the seat of our metal gazebo. Having caught my breath, I looked up, breathed deeply, and tried to relax.

A delightful maroon and yellow apparition appeared as my eyes started to focus on what was in front of me. It was a magnificent maroon and yellow Bearded Iris that had obviously just bloomed. I felt the Lord whisper to my heart: "Just for you."

I felt a frisson go right through me.

Thank you, Lord. What a beautiful gift!

You have no doubt been on walks when you have noticed amazing cloud formations. Sometimes they look like angelic hosts, at other times they tend to resemble less pleasant beings, maybe even huge, demonic beasts. At times, the sunlight will filter through the clouds in such a way that it really affects you. A few minutes later, you might return to exactly the same spot and all the wonderful formations have disappeared.

They were put there just for you at that very moment. What an amazing, awesome God we have.

He is totally breathtaking.

Even though Jesus knew that He could heal and revive Lazarus, He still wept when He heard that Lazarus had died.

The Scriptures say that the Lord is compassionate and close to the brokenhearted[14] and that our names are inscribed on the palms of His hand.[15]

It is beautiful to know that Jesus weeps with us, that He is close in our pain. He has sent the Holy Spirit to be with us, to bring comfort. Many find solace in that, and so they should.

If I am honest though, I prefer to have Jesus take the pain from me. Or that He distracts me, which He often does. When I call out to Jesus, something usually distracts me from my circumstances. It might be the telephone; music may come on or the news breaks in. Life and laughter are distractions, and they promote pain relief.

Sometimes, when I am stuck say, on a chair or on my bed, I pray, and the Lord eventually provides a solution. He will either send an invisible angel to assist me by helping me up, or Ben will suddenly turn up to lend a hand.

If you are wondering about the invisible angel holding me up, I will explain. When getting up, I often have a great deal of difficulty, especially when my dopamine levels are low. At those times, if there is no one around to help, I pray for angelic assistance. I do not actually see an angel, even in the spirit. Usually what happens is that, as I endeavour to hoist myself up a bit, I feel a steadying in my body, and I feel secure enough and strong enough to become fully upright. It is very subtle.

I encourage you, my dear reader, to ask for angelic assistance whenever you need it. I understand that not enough people ask for that type of help and there are many unemployed angels around.

I have designed a house in my mind, where I would like to live in heaven. Jesus is quoted in John's Gospel, chapter 14 as saying, "In my house there are many mansions."

Some people believe we will have our own homes in Heaven. It matters not. An imaginary house in Heaven will benefit us now.

My heavenly home has a cottage garden managed by angels. The furniture is of handcrafted timber. There are lacy curtains. The air is crisp and cool, as you would find in our local Dandenong Ranges.

There is a veranda which encircles the timber home. A staircase leads directly from the front door to the front lawn, Queenslander style. There is a rose arbour and a quince tree. I have sat in the Spirit with Jesus in the kitchen, sharing large, warm scones with Him with coddled cream, the absolute best of homemade raspberry jam and a pot of English Breakfast Tea. The Lord then seems to lead me to a place where I could smell and touch the freshly baked scones that positively melted in my mouth.

Now this did not happen in the physical world. It was in my imagination. It was in my spirit. I did not ask for it. The scene unfolded as I sat with the Lord.

Ask the Lord for similar encounters. He will design them just for you because He loves you. He wants to put a smile on your face. He knows what you need and what would delight just you, His precious treasure.

Jesus promised that He would be with us, even to the end of the world.[16]

Currently, at the time of writing, 200 people are held hostage in Gaza. Thirty of these are children.

The call is for people to adopt one child each and pray for them for comfort, for a miraculous rescue, for them to find their Messiah, that they may experience joy and find favour with their captives.

Hopefully, they will all be rescued.

I am praying for angelic assistance for all the hostages.

# *Interlude*

Think about your thought life for a moment. Then read the scriptures below.

Since you have been raised to new life with Christ, set your sights on the realities of heaven, where Christ sits in the place of honour at God's right hand. Think about the things of heaven, not the things of earth. For you died to this life, and your real life is hidden with Christ in God.
Colossians 3 :1 to 3 (NLT)

And now, dear brothers and sisters, one final thing. Fix your eyes on what is true, and honourable, and right, and pure, and lovely and admirable.
Philippians 4:8 (NLT)

# Prayer

*Loveliest Lord, all glory and honour be to You.*
*You are the Lamb that was slain and the Lion of Judah.*
*We surrender our whole selves to You, Glorious One!*

# 13

## The Comfort Of His Presence

I love reading about Dietrich Bonhoeffer, a Christian pastor who plotted against Hitler during the Second World War. He was executed close to the end of the war.

He found even his days in prison to be most satisfying. He ministered to the guards, counselling and praying for them. The Lord always gives us opportunities to do His work, no matter what our circumstances.

Bonhoeffer also wrote that he could feel the prayers of his intercessors lifting him up.

The Lord took me aside after church one Sunday and reiterated to me that He will never let us suffer beyond what we can bear. If the suffering seemed to be intolerable, it might be because of a wrong heart attitude like, for example, not surrendering to the Lord or holding on to pride, instead of embracing humility.

There are so many examples of the Lord making Himself manifest to people in their suffering.

My husband had a very serious bike accident in his teenage years. He was not a believer back then. It was his mother who later told him that when she visited him in hospital, soon after the accident, Ben had shared with her that he was never left alone. He said that someone was always there with him in the hospital, keeping him company.

By the time he recovered, he had forgotten about that experience until he was reminded of it many years later, when he had become a believer.

The knowledge that Ben was never left alone probably comforted his mother more than him.

## *Interlude*

Read Psalm 139.

The Lord knows every thought before we think it.
He knows everything about us.
He knew all the suffering we would face,
and He went ahead to carefully prepare the way.

Can you imagine what that means?
**Take a moment to let that truth sink in.**

We might have been surprised, but He was not taken unawares by any means. He has put everything and everybody in place to help us cope. That would include our carers, friends, family, and health professionals. Sometimes I pinch myself because I am so amazed by the glory, compassion, and foresight of God. I certainly feel blessed that I have had such a skilled and insightful medical team, which includes my physiotherapist, occupational therapist, neurologist, and the list goes on.

# Prayer

*What love is this, O Lord, that You truly are with us always.*
*You are indeed always with us, comforting,*
*humouring, entertaining, loving.*
*We thank You for this wondrous gift.*

# 14

## Playful Surprises

There are countless ways that He endeavours to put a smile on our faces. We have to have eyes to see this and appreciate the love that is behind His creative ways.

Ask Him for those eyes. He will give them to you.

In the middle of September 2023, I was sitting with the Lord, waiting for some revelation when I had a vision of a black and white cake.

It took me a minute or so to grasp what this might mean. I knew the last weekend in September was coming up. This was usually the weekend of our Melbourne Australian Rules football grand final.

I didn't even know which teams were playing. I am not a close follower of football. My team, the Mighty Magpies, are so rarely in the grand final.

They won a grand final in 1990, twelve months after I had given my heart to the Lord. I remember joking back then, that the Lord might have arranged that win as a special congratulatory gift for me.

Their colours are black and white. Just like the cake I had seen.

Perhaps the cake was pointing to another grand final win?

Well, I immediately checked out the teams that would be playing. They were indeed Collingwood and Brisbane. I was definitely going to be watching them play.

Once the game began, I started to pray. The Lord seemed to be saying that I needed to intercede in order to make sure that they won. I prayed all the way through,

Well, what a game it was! I could sense the Lord's joy in all of this. One team would be a few points ahead of the other. Then the other would catch up and they would be neck to neck for a while.

Again, one team would kick a goal or two, then mine would catch up. All this went on for about three hours. My team won by a few points!

That result brought so much joy to so many people. Many Collingwood supporters emerged from their closets that day.

How privileged did I feel that Collingwood had featured in my vision. That is the sort of God we serve. I did not ask the Lord for that revelation. It was simply a playful gift.

# Interlude

**Do not despise these small beginnings,
for the Lord rejoices to see the work begin.**
Zechariah 4:10 (NLT)

This scripture refers to the rebuilding of the Temple after the Jews returned from their exile in Babylon.

The Lord recently highlighted it to me, last week in fact, as it also referred to my health. He reminded me of all the little ways in which He had been improving my symptoms. A couple of years ago, I could not touch the floor to pick anything up. Now I can. I am incredibly grateful for that.

I used to get dyskinesia - embarrassing, jerky movements caused by the levodopa medicine. That has gone.

I used to call out loudly in my sleep and even fall out of bed quite regularly. That has stopped.

*I am sorry, Lord, that I have despised these small improvements, and I have not taken the time to thank you for them. Thank you, Jesus! I worship and adore You.*

How about you, dear reader, is there work the Lord has been doing that you have not taken the time to acknowledge?

# Prayer

*Precious Saviour, I thank You for the many things you have done for me.
I know that You are looking out for me, every minute of every day.
Such knowledge is too wonderful for me.*

# PART THREE

# UNPACKING THE ARTISAN'S TOOLS

# 15

## Humour

I like to imagine that, with my diagnosis, the Lord entrusted me with an ancient treasure chest full of artisan's tools, instruments, and keys.

These are precious utensils that have been known since ancient times to be most effective in times of trouble.

Let us unpack these.

I am not going to put them in any kind of order. That would only lead to some foolish arguments, angst, and hot air.

Every minute of every day will require various kinds of assistance.

This morning, Lyn and I, in a spurt of spontaneity, dashed down to a quaint local bakery and treated ourselves to some lovely cake. We were served some magnificent Danish pastries with custard and lots of raspberries, finished off with a gigantic dollop of the best humour.

Of course, we ended up dissolving in raucous laughter. Why? Because of my failing fine motor skills. I just did not cope with the considerable challenge of balancing the fine raspberries on top of the custard filled Danish. That failure left me with a giant, bright red stain on the thigh of my tracksuit pants.

Often, in those moments, I announce that I am a science student, testing whether gravity is working as well as it should.

To laugh or to cry? It was 10.15 am and we were about to embark on our morning of painting. We chose laughter, grit, and determination. How dare anything get in our way this morning! A bright red stain only confirms that the pants are ideal for painting!

It ended up being the start of a fun-filled morning. People were chatty, old, favourite classmates turned up unexpectedly and comments were made about the freedom in our giving up control and just having a good laugh.

Some weeks ago, I asked Lyn, in the interest of including motivational content in this book, what made her get up in the morning.

She gave me a quirky look. I think I read her mind when I answered for her.

"It's your bladder, isn't it?" She grinned sheepishly.

Recently Ben and I were sitting in a McDonalds café in a country town, on our road trip to Queensland. It was a time when the Lord was training me to see better in the spirit.

I was delighted that Jesus opened my eyes to see Him seated opposite me. I saw Him with my spiritual eyes. My physical eyes were not involved at all.

With a huge smile on His face, Jesus began juggling with coloured balls. It was so very funny that I started laughing and laughing. It was such a privilege.

Humour will take us all quite a distance! Humour feeds the spirit. Let us embrace it as a marvellous gift, always to be celebrated and enjoyed.

Our dear Jesus is a man with a great sense of humour. I love the reference to His joy in Psalm 45:

**Your God has anointed you, (Jesus)**
**Pouring out the oil of joy on you**
**More than on anyone else.**
Psalm 45:7 (NLT) (*Emphasis added*)

# Interlude

Think about the last time you had a good laugh.
Try to remember a good joke or even make one up.

# Prayer

*Dearest Lord, thank you for humour.*
*Laughter is superb medicine, as your Word says.*
*Please develop my sense of humour even further,*
*so that I can spread Your joy to others, wherever I go.*

# 16

# Brakes And Self-Nurture

Let us dip into our treasure chest again. What else is in there that will be of great use? A set of well-maintained brakes, of course!!

Why brakes, you say?

Because you will need to slow down. Considerably. It is no good trying to run through life. In is no good trying to hide from the suffering. It is best to turn towards it and face it head on. The Lord is holding our hands. He even holds us up and carries us. Be willing to allow other, trusted souls to carry you as well.

Slow down to a very gentle pace, so that you can appreciate all that the Lord has placed around you.

Savour the delights of flowers, be entranced by the play of light on trees, leaves, and buildings.

Drink deep of all the beautiful fragrances that you can track down. These might emanate from trees and flowers, or maybe from fresh or cooked culinary delights.

Let chocolate and vanilla be sources of immense pleasure.

Getting out into the bushland can be very soothing and uplifting. When you choose to go for a walk, ask yourself where the most soothing place would be to go that is within reach.

As you fumble around in your tool kit, be mindful that, lying at the very bottom of your treasure chest, you will discover a large round golden container labelled *Capacity for Self-love and Self-nurture*. You will need it. Take excellent care of it.

We are strengthening our own spirits to ensure that they are up to the task of caring for our body, mind and soul.

This is different from selfishness. It is the task of being good stewards of the body, soul and spirit with which the Lord has entrusted us.

Spend time exploring the nooks and crannies of your life to discover and/or re-discover interests and hobbies that build you up.

Then cram your eye-catching toolbox with many encouraging and calming activities that you can access whenever you might fancy indulging in them.

Some examples of delightful hobbies can be looking at old photographs and letters, painting, knitting and crochet, woodwork, music, singing, watching films, board games, bocce, croquet, cooking, or brewing. There are many more. The possibilities are endless.

Never be critical of anything that you produce. As an antidote to suffering, you will need complete freedom of expression. Do not let anyone rob you of the delights of creativity. Send the harsh judgments of others to the pit. Don't even ask for the opinion of others unless they are totally trustworthy.

Others do not necessarily have your best interests at heart. They can be insecure, jealous, or impatient – there are many unhelpful motivating factors. Again, put your self- love and self-nurture to work.

Meanwhile. An essential spray can in your instrument box is the 'abuse repellent'. Do not tolerate abuse. Even if you have to shout loudly at your abuser, using the words, "No abuse, you goose!"

Abusers are mostly operating out of cowardice or, at best, ignorance. If your repellent does not work, get outside help.

# Interlude

Name something you are passionate about.
Ask the Lord to help you find it.
Make sure your toolkit is never without 'Other centredness.
Always find room to help others,
even if it is only with an encouraging email or text message.
Your helpfulness will help them and then wash back onto you,
and you will eventually also be blessed.

# Prayer

*Precious Heavenly Father, show me how very much You love me, so that I can learn from Your example and extend that love to those around me and even to show great kindness to myself, in my struggle.*

# 17

## Pleasure And Leisure

In those dark days after Black Saturday, Rob Gordon, a Melbourne psychologist specialising in trauma recovery, gave several public talks on practical things we could do to recover. This applied whether we had lost people, property, or both.

His focus on "Pleasure and Leisure" is useful for all types of suffering. We all need time out, away from the suffering, for recuperation, even for an hour.

Rather than seeing pleasure and leisure as self-indulgence, we have to begin to see it as a kind of medicine that must be taken regularly in order to be effective.

Rob Gordon stressed the importance of this. He insisted that we all give ourselves permission to regularly undertake "Pleasure and Leisure" activities.

There are many uplifting activities to choose from. They can be as simple as chatting to an uplifting friend on the phone, watching a favourite movie or playing sport. It must be an activity that feeds our soul, lifts us up and provides a distraction. However, we should try to avoid alcohol and excessive eating. A glass of wine, a piece of chocolate cake and/or some ice-cream are all fine in moderation.

How often should we undertake "Pleasure and Leisure?"

Regularly! Once a day would be good or, at least once per week. I go out for coffee with a friend. Sometimes even looking at cakes can be therapeutic!

I also wander into the garden, looking for things that have grown or flowered. The Lord loves the garden as well. It is awesome to meet Him there.

Apart from the Lord, you can be your own best friend. Find your passion. Be kind to yourself. If you do not have a passion, ask the Lord for one or two or even three.

Mine became painting and music and composing. And writing.

It can be swimming, gardening, or drawing. The drawing classes I attend with Lyn at a local library are free, creative and most fulfilling.

You certainly do not have to be good at any of these activities. I am certainly not good at them. They still give me pleasure, though. I do not compare myself with anyone else and neither welcome, nor even listen to, any negative comments.

# Interlude

Ask the Lord for a suggestion of a fun thing to do either by yourself, with Him or with others.

Then go and actually do it.

# Prayer

*Sweetest Lord, I need help to adequately nurture myself at the moment.*
*Please guide me. Show me how to schedule in this healthy*
*and uplifting activity.*
*In the name of Yeshua, the Messiah, I pray.*

# 18

# The Secret Place

There is no doubt that the only way to maintain or develop a relationship with someone is to spend time with them. It can be a little trickier if the Person is invisible. Nevertheless, Jesus is a person like any other, and like no other.

I would suggest that you do not be legalistic about it. Do not be guilt-ridden if you miss some time with Him. Just persist, and there will be a time of sudden breakthrough.

The secret place is where He equips us, strengthens us for the journey and where our friendship with the Lord is knitted together.

Often it is hard to get there. There are so many little distractions.

If you feel clueless about starting, take heart, because I felt the same way when I began.

I found it immensely helpful to set aside a seat or even a small room in the house which I particularly liked and could reserve for myself. Because that seat was used exclusively for prayer time, I found it easier to pray after just a few days. It started to have a peaceful atmosphere around it, making it easier to connect with Jesus and the Holy Spirit.

Don't forget to take the time to patiently listen to the Lord and write down what you hear.

He needs a listening ear just like we do.

As far as Bible reading is concerned, Psalms and Proverbs are a great start. I try to read one Psalm a day and a chapter of Proverbs.

There are 31 chapters in the Book of Proverbs - one for each day of the month.

Whenever I feel stuck, I read Psalm 145, which is filled with wonderful praise. It never fails to uplift me towards the Lord. Try reading it.

I think the morning is the best time to set aside a bit of quiet time. Not a morning person? The ninth hour, or 3pm is an excellent time. But let's face it, any time is the right time.

Spending time with the Lord is a living experience. Sometimes it goes very smoothly. Sometimes you have to press in, persist, and be dogged about it.

I try to spend at least an hour with the Lord each day in total. It may be 15 minutes at a time, depending on my spasms and other uncomfortable distractions. On a bad day, I just give the Lord a wave, as if to say, "Thinking of you! Sending love your way!" It is easy to forget that Jesus is fully human.

And He is fully God as well.

An hour sounds like a lot to begin with, but it gets easier as time goes by.

I configure that time as I please, as long as it includes things like:

- A Bible Reading
- Going through a list of people or issues in my life that I want to pray for. I mainly pray that my family to be saved and/or healed. I mention them by name.
- Time just sitting with the Lord in silence.
- Asking the Lord what is on His heart.
- Praying for other causes, such as our church, our State, the war in Israel.
- Worship and thanks.

These things easily fill in an hour. Some days I mostly read the Bible and on other days I just sit quietly. I keep a journal nearby to jot down pictures I see, dreams, verses in the Bible, or other words the Lord gives me from time to time.

After a few months it is fun to see if the words I receive from the Lord come true.

Sometimes I can really feel the Lord's presence with me. That makes praying much easier. However, I have to keep in mind that the Enemy is always trying to upset my time with the Lord, so I do not complain if I do not sense His beautiful presence. I just persist. Singing or playing worship songs can help. Gratitude prayers, where I think of all the little things that I am grateful for, help me to get into the right frame of mind. Set prayers, like the Lord's prayer, can also help.

You can pray any scripture as well and make the words apply to you, like this:

> **Lord, I pray that I may have power,**
> **together with all the Lord's**
> **holy people, to grasp how wide**
> **and long and high and deep is Your love.**
> Ephesians 3:18 (NIV)

Persistence is vital. We have to use sheer grit, as if we are training for a sporting competition.

What do I do when I am sitting with the Lord? I just concentrate on loving him. He turns up. Not always straight away, but He is worth waiting for.

Remember, His manifest presence is a bonus. If you have to sit with Him without that peaceful sense of Him being alongside you, make that your gift to Him. He deserves it.

*Interlude*

Spend the next five minutes just sitting with the Lord in silence.

# Prayer

*Lord, I so want to develop our friendship in the secret place.*
*I totally rely on You to help me play my part.*
*I love You, Lord.*

# 19

## The Vibrancy Of Colour

Colours can be a source of great comfort. When I started painting in my crude, rigid style, I noticed that certain colours began to bring me consolation and stimulation. Give them a try. Try drawing, painting, collage or colouring in books. I know all too well that many people are reluctant to pick up a paintbrush. It has something to do with critical words spoken by someone, about our art.

Exploring art requires a level of courage and cheek. I will let you in on a secret - just about everyone experiences some level of insecurity when it comes to art.

Personally, I say be bold, nurture that self-love hidden within you, and explore whatever medium gives you the greatest pleasure. Remember, no self-evaluation is allowed. Just enjoy the texture of the paint and the vibrancy of the colours. We have people in our "Playing with Painting" group who love the structure and order of the colouring books. As I observe them, I notice they are getting bolder all the time. Each week they become more daring in their choice and juxtaposition of the colours. Others, especially those with brain malfunction, go for total vibrancy of colour. There are, of course, many in our group who are on the spectrum. I would love to see them liberated.

I love the freedom of paint as it flows quite easily without needing any fine motor control. Fine motor control is my weakest point. I do love the freedom of the splashed bomb of paint.

I have not developed any major technical skills, but I love the very act of painting. I love the feel of the paint going onto the canvas. The games one can play with watercolour paint and good quality water-colour paper! The merging colours fascinate me. I have learned to be totally uncritical and just enjoy the process. Oftentimes, I am pleasantly surprised by the result. It is truly therapeutic to paint.

There is so much joy to be found loading colour onto a brush, whether it be acrylic, oil or watercolour. There is something about the easy flow that is exhilarating and comforting at the same time.

Again, let me reiterate, the key is to leave self-criticism behind. Do not show your work to anyone unless you trust them implicitly. Others can crush your confidence early on, or even later in life. You need the freedom to experiment without being accountable to anyone else. Just explore your own creativity.

## *Interlude*

Find some coloured pencils, crayons or pastels and a piece of paper. Pick the colour that you like best today. Do a stick figure drawing of yourself and underneath it write the words, "I like you". We need to love ourselves just as the Lord loves us. Self-acceptance is key.

**I look to the mountains where does my help come from**
**My help comes from the Lord who made heaven and earth**.
Psalm 121:1-2 (NIV)

My life is up and down in more than one aspect, so I have to rely on the Lord moment by moment, more so than other people who can be reasonably confident about being able to walk and talk tomorrow.

# Prayer

*Almighty Creator, thank you for sharing the joy of creating with us,*
*Your children.*
*Grant us the freedom and boldness to create like You!*

# 20

# The Secret Chord

I am very intrigued by the story of David and his secret chord which he used when he played the harp for Saul to soothe his pain. I certainly find music to be therapeutic. When I cannot move, I try to play my little harpika or kalimba.

How do the sounds they produce give me immense joy? The music sets off the neurotransmitters in my brain and I can move better.

I also have a piano and a keyboard, for when I really want to let loose. I truly recommend that people acquire some type of instrument to play a chord or melody to make a little music. I have a little tin whistle for squeakier sounds. I use all my instruments to help me compose little tunes that improve my mood and my movement. I also like writing lyrics, especially for all types of worship.

I am no whiz kid. I just do what pleases me. I do not have to please anyone else. So, I explore music and any other type of creativity that appeals to me at the time. Sometimes in the morning, when I cannot move, I will get out my little instruments. I have memorised some songs that I like, some of which are self-composed. They certainly bring me a lot of pleasure and relax my whole being. They are a fun activity that takes my mind off myself, even if only for a little while. Persist and you will find something that works for you.

I had convinced myself that I was totally tone deaf and could not sing in tune and would never play an instrument.

If you have never played a musical instrument, like for example a piano, it is only a matter of not having done so YET. It does not mean that you are not musical or somehow genetically incapable of playing.

That is a lie that we baby boomers were taught when we were growing up.

I did some singing lessons in my late sixties and found that my vocal range is definitely not great. However, music can be transposed to suit one's vocal range, to an extent. I can now play very basic piano which cheers me up. Although there is room for much improvement, I compose little pieces of music that make me smile.

Music really does bring healing to the soul and movement back to my body.

This discovery reminds me so much of King David's secret chord, which has become quite famous through Leonard Cohen's famous song "Hallelujah."

David would play the harp when an evil spirit afflicted Saul. This would make Saul feel better.

We can read about it in 1 Samuel 16:23, **And whenever the evil spirit came upon Saul, David took the lyre and played it with his hand, and Saul would feel better, and the evil spirit would depart from him.**

# *Interlude*

Spend two minutes thinking about your favourite song or piece of music.
Perhaps listen to it if you feel so inclined.

Read Chapters 1 and 2 of John's Gospel.

# Prayer

*Lord, I love the splendour of music. I stand in awe when I think about all the gifted composers throughout history.*
*You totally amaze me, Heavenly Father!*

Isn't God good that He orchestrates life like this? He mercifully brings so much light into a dark world.

Just as I typed the last sentence, my husband brought in a full punnet's worth of juicy, sweet, home-grown strawberries. The timing is delightful. When we believe life is like boiled turnip, the Lord gladdens our hearts with joyful berries! Praise to the Almighty One.

# 21

# Trash Can

We already have a treasure box filled with wonderful artisan's tools. As with every renovation, there will be things to throw onto the rubbish pile.

What should we discard in the midst of our suffering?

We have focussed on what we need to hang on to and carefully keep handy in our toolbox.

Let us turn our focus to what is going to be relegated to the trash can.

To start with, fill the trash can with all the judgments you have ever made against yourself. As people, we can be horribly self-effacing and harshly judge our performance as a parent, spouse, student, or worker. We need to tell the Lord we are sorry, and then imagine shredding all those judgements.

Second on the list are the judgements we have made of other people. I had a pile of judgments I needed to repent of. I have judged people, including myself, since I was a teenager. I foolishly thought it was a sign of cleverness. I certainly made a lot of people laugh with my derisive comments of others. Such an attitude by no means pleases the Lord!

Take a moment to reflect on your judgements. I found that I judged my parents, teachers, politicians and many more. I found that I feel much better when I extend grace to everyone in my life, asking for the Lord's help, and for His forgiveness.

> *I am so sorry, Lord for judging myself and others. And so harshly, too.*
> *And often just for a laugh or two. Please forgive me, Lord.*

Did you know that it is true that we reap what we sow? I have seen many examples of this. For example, if you judge someone else for having unruly children, you may find that your children, too, will be hard to discipline.

If you think through all the people in your life, you will probably find similar examples.

We will be judged in the same harsh way that we judge others. Yes, it is true. So let us repent, and the sooner the better.

Manipulation can also go straight to the incinerator. Manipulation is a very unsavoury way to exert your will over others. Apologise to the Lord.

> *I am sorry that I have used manipulation to exert my will, Lord.*
> *Please forgive me.*

Do you know what 'bitter root judgements' are? They are when you make sad and bitter predictions like, "People always ignore me" or "I never get my fair share."

Those predictions invariably come true. If you say people always ignore you, you will find that they do. They will not pay attention to you until you repent of the judgement you have made.

After repenting, it would be good if you declared the opposite for example, "People listen to me as I have worthwhile things to say. Lord, give me wisdom and the right motivation when I speak."

I have to confess that I have found myself feeling compelled to ignore some people, whether I want to or not. Then I later discovered that they had made this vow.

Tell the Lord you are sorry for your bitter root judgments and speak out the opposite - speak out a positive prediction that nullifies the bitter one.

For example, turn, "People always ignore me" into, "I will not deliberately ignore anyone who needs my attention. People certainly do not ignore me. Teach me kindness and humility, sweet Saviour of mine."

Throw the following words straight into the bin:

"Should," "must", "need to", "have to", "shouldn't", "mustn't".

The last thing you need is to feel obligated. Ask the Lord to clarify what He wants you to do today. Some days are productive. Others are not. Guilt is totally unhelpful.

Ask Jesus for His peace. Find rest for your soul. Whatever you do, do it from a place of rest. Then you are more likely to be clearheaded and effective.

## Interlude

Write down three things you want to throw onto the rubbish pile
and then tear up and throw away the piece of paper.

# Prayer

*Lord, I invite you into all aspects of my life.*
*Welcome, Lord Jesus, into my whole being.*
*Teach me your godly ways. Purify my heart, O Lord.*

# 22

# The Call

By now you would have had a decent look at the contents of your toolbox, and you will have filled your trash can with all the things that are unhelpful.

Just remember your regular, spiritual medication:

- Pleasure and leisure
- Conversation with your Creator
- A large dose of Holy Spirit power as often as required.

You decide the dosage. You decide the frequency.

When we receive a nasty diagnosis, our minds turn to the future, and we wonder what changes we are going to be facing.

I eventually retired from paid work. I am pleased, however, that the Lord continued to call me into new things, despite my illness.

In my neighbouring town of Lilydale, for which I have quite a bit of passion, we had been waiting for many years for a community centre to open.

When it was finally launched after the Covid lockdown, I was beside myself with enthusiasm. I quickly busied myself, teaching a bit of English as a Second Language. I also founded a German group focusing on German language and culture. Baking German cakes such as Marmorkuchen[17] and even Berliner became a big feature of my life for a while.

Although I really love to paint, it is quite a struggle for me to produce something that I like. However, the Lord wanted me to start this "Playing with Paint" group.

While sitting in a craft group with a dear lady who was knitting in the most vibrant colours, I came up with the idea of a "Playing with Paint" group.

You have to realise that I was that girl in the art class at school who got extremely poor marks in the practical side of art. My pieces were very rarely put on display. My art teacher looked at me quizzically one day and shook her head, "You really don't enjoy art, do you?" She could not work out how anyone could prefer Maths to Art. I certainly did.

Anyway, getting back to the new painting group, I asked around for assistance, but no friend or acquaintance of mine shared an interest in combining painting with evangelism.

Fortunately, the coordinator of the community house saw the value in starting such a group. There had certainly been some enthusiasm for the group evident amongst the knitters. I felt that, especially people like me who had problems with their brains, would benefit from experimenting with colour. Somehow colour seemed to 'flick switches' on and off in my brain, releasing energy and joy.

Finally, the day came for it to start. In trepidation, I packed some painting gear and trotted down to the centre, not knowing what to expect.

To my great joy and relief, a Christian lady who is a professional artist and whom I had met at the centre about a month earlier, was one of the first to arrive. What a relief. I introduced her to the other students as the expert, should they need any technical assistance.

# Prayer

*Dearest Lord, please show us what assignments and callings You still have for us, in the midst of this time of trial.*

# 23

## Grief And Loss

**Blessed are those who mourn,**
**for they will be comforted.**
Matthew 5:4 (NIV)

We frequently encounter grief and loss in their many forms and disguises. Loss of a job or ministry, a breakdown of a friendship or the inability to have another child. All of these engender feelings of grief and loss.

We can experience the grief of loss when circumstances change, like when a colleague resigns. Often it comes quite suddenly.

The day my brother died, I was having a BBQ. You can see the dark humour, can't you?

I had invited a new work colleague over, members of my family and some friends.

Miraculously, all went superbly well in terms of food preparation and the fact that the guests appeared to be enjoying themselves.

I usually had a lot of anxiety when I invited people over. I feared they would have nothing to say to me or each other, or that the food would be inedible or not ready on time.

On the morning of the Sunday, 8th February 2009, all the preparations went swimmingly. I kept questioning myself, "Why is everything going so well? Have I finally had a 'breakthrough' in the area of hospitality?"

When my friends arrived at the door, they looked very worried.

"Have you heard about Marysville? Thank God everyone was rescued. Is your brother all right?"

My brother David Sebald and his wife Marlene owned the real estate agency in Marysville at the time of the tragic fires of 2009.

I had no idea that my brother had been in any sort of danger. There had been fires, but they had centred around Kilmore, which was a very long way away.

Louise went on to explain that Marysville had burnt down, the fire having changed direction the night before and had raged through Marysville like a firestorm.

"But don't worry," Louise added, "they all assembled at the footy oval and are down in Buxton."

I expected to hear from my brother. If a fire had come through and he was camping out in Buxton, surely he would tell us.

I rang his phone several times. After my guests left, I started to call the Red Cross, to find out if he had registered with them. I had established that this is what happens in these types of situations.

The phone calls were fruitless. One of David and Marlene's friends had my number and we spoke every couple of hours, in case one or the other had some news.

Finally, I flopped into bed and tried not to think about the fires anymore.

Then, at about 6am, I woke up with a knowing beyond knowing in my stomach, that David had indeed died.

I found my way to the office, expecting to get some kind of confirmation that morning.

Sure enough, mid-morning, one of David's staff at his real estate agency called me to tell me that David and Marlene had died in their home on the evening of Saturday, 7 February 2009. It was what we later called "Black Saturday".

What many people do not realise is that traumatic grief is quite different from the 'usual' grief. An unexpected death, either from a tragedy like a plane crash, fire, flood, or earthquake, releases a profound grief within the surviving family which does not heal quickly. If it is in the public eye, like Black Saturday was, the survivors are reminded day after day of their loss as they watch the news. People ask after them and remind them constantly. Then there are the anniversaries, which bring the whole tragedy to mind, yet again.

There was an upside to having lost David and Marlene so publicly. Trauma counsellors were made available to us, and educational events were held to assist us in dealing with our pain. Support groups were formed as the grief lasted much longer than normal grief - four to five years at least, compared to half that time for losing a parent or spouse in the usual course of events.

The main things I learned were:

Firstly, to 'go with' the grief and not fight it. I learned to let it 'wash over me,' which was appropriate because it came in waves. I learned to allow myself to 'feel' the sadness, not to run away from it. The sadness had a value in itself, if only to help us realise how much the people in our lives mean to us. If we were not sad when we lost our brothers, our sisters-in-law, or any other family members or friends, then they could not have meant much to us.

Secondly, the counsellors taught us that we needed to be kind to ourselves. Just as there is value in feeling sad, there is also value in feeding our souls with things that nurtured us. Things like walks along the beach or through the forest. Things like playing our very favourite music or going out for ice cream or coffee. To be our own best friend, in a sense. To find out what feeds our souls and then to go ahead and feed them. Baking cookies, playing with the dog, watching our favourite movie yet again, became things that were great for our mental and emotional wellbeing. By no means ought we to see them as extravagant time wasters. All these things are not luxuries, but food for the soul. Necessary for survival. These activities ware part of an insurance policy against depression.

Thirdly, we were also taught to keep an eye on our intake of nutrients. Frozen vegetables, for example, were seen as a straightforward source of vitamins.

I applied these important lessons when I was diagnosed with Parkinson's. That is why I have a mind map in my kitchen, reminding me of all the things I love to do. These include socialising, playing music, painting, writing, and composing. I do not claim to be particularly skilled in any of these pursuits. I just enjoy doing them.

I do not have too much advice for you in your grief, except to say, as I pointed out earlier, slowing down is especially important. Talk about your loss. Talk about your memories.

Be aware that you may be tempted to undertake risk-taking behaviours or do things that appear to be out of character. One thing I did was organise a bush camping trip in the middle of winter. It was lovely to spend time with family. It was not particularly dangerous, but it was, of course, extremely cold. When you are grieving, you want to be reminded that you are truly alive. I think that is the explanation for the risk taking.

# *Interlude*

Stand up, if you can, or move in your wheelchair
to a window or door. In your mind's eye,
try to imagine whom or what
you would like to see on the other side
of the window or door.

Focus on that picture for 20 seconds.

# Prayer

*Lord, help me to face my losses.*
*Give me the courage to stay when the temptation is to flee from the pain.*
*I trust You, Lord Jesus to be everything I need in this season of my life.*

# 24

# This Present Age

In the next world, the tears will be wiped from our eyes[18] but in this world there will be trouble.

What is trouble? A mild cold? A scarcity of parking spaces?

The Greek word used in John's Gospel means distress.[19] "Thlipsis", in the Greek, "tsar" in Hebrew – affliction, distress.

In John 16:33 Jesus tells us, **"But be of good cheer, for I have overcome (a continuous and abiding victory) the world."**

It is not a glib, easy victory. It takes persistence and it looks different each time. The word for trouble Jesus uses in this passage is used to describe the turmoil caused by being tied up with a rope and having a weighty rock placed on our chest. The rock is so heavy it would crush our bones. A bit like when the road runner drops a rock on the coyote in that cartoon we baby boomers watched in our youngest years.

We also have to remember that one day, we will live in glory with Jesus.

He does restore what the locusts have eaten.[20]

In this present age there are particular types of suffering that may have escaped our attention earlier, or they simply did not exist.

Since the pandemic, I have noticed a descent into lawlessness and disorder. There appear to be more computer outages and problems with government departments. Or it may be that I am becoming less tolerant of those things ...

## *Interlude*

Spend five minutes planning a fun activity for next week.

Read Chapter 3 of John's Gospel.

# Prayer

*Heavenly Father, let me be of good cheer.*
*Let me be a clear and bright beacon of light in these dark times.*
*I would like to lead many into Your truth.*
*That is the will of my heart, dearest Saviour.*

# 25

## Persecution

In his second letter to the Thessalonians, Paul says that the man of lawlessness will be revealed in the last days.

There is no doubt that this is a time of increasing lawlessness. At the same time, a spiritual awakening is meant to be starting in Australia as I write this. It is prophesied to be coming down from Toowoomba in Queensland, and then going in all directions across this land.

There are people in my church who are 'on their faces' (meaning that many are humbling themselves in prayer, kneeling, lying prostrate, taking on a humble posture), before the Lord several times a week.

Hand in hand with the lawlessness, will come increasing power and authority in the body of Christ. The purpose of the power and authority will be to enable us to overcome the larger obstacles that we will be facing. It will be a spiritual battle on a higher level.

The whole book of Revelation is pointing in this direction.

Revelation 14:12 in the New Living Translation states, **"God's holy people must endure persecution patiently, obeying his commands and maintaining their faith in Jesus."**

In the Book of Revelation, the Lord is encouraging us to endure, and He talks about an unleashing of evil. The book is replete with uplifting visions of Heaven and the next life, and also the apocalyptic visions of immense evil.

What about us? Will there be a rapture? Will we be scooped up suddenly, in the blink of an eye, to be with the Lord, meeting Him in the air?

I am comforted by Matthew 24:21, where Jesus is talking about the Tribulation that is to occur before He returns. They are words of consolation.

**"For there will be greater anguish than at any time since the world began. And it will never be so great again. In fact, unless that calamity is shortened, not a single person will survive. But it will be shortened for the sake of God's chosen ones."** (NLT)

To further encourage us, John, in Revelation, writes about the rewards for those who endure and overcome.

Metaphorically, we need to jump into the arms of Jesus. He will surely be with us until the "end of the age."

Our lives need to continue with meaning and purpose. We need to have the right attitudes in our hearts and minds to help us persevere when suffering comes. We need to be reassured that we are not alone. We need to comprehend that we are loved and not abandoned. Those of us who suffer, need to be secure in the knowledge that we are still worthwhile people, even though we are not able to contribute as much to society when we are incapacitated.

We long for our bodies to be released from sin and suffering. We "wait with eager hope" for the new bodies He has promised us.[21]

# Prayer

*Lord, we need You so much in these troubled times.*
*Strengthen us.*
*Give us great wisdom and compassion for the lost.*

# PART FOUR

# A VISION AND
# TWO DREAMS

# 26

# Losses

Parkinson's is a neurodegenerative disease, which means that the symptoms are expected to get worse.

I trusted and prayed that mine would not deteriorate. Certainly, my mind has remained quite sharp, although I have complaints about my memory, along with everyone else my age (I am turning 70 in a couple of months).

During the course of writing this book my body has certainly stiffened up some more and physical tasks are getting harder and harder.

I have stopped planning new activities in case I have to cancel at the last minute. My face has stiffened, so it is set in a stiff, unfriendly expression, as if the wind had changed while I was angry. People ask me if there is something wrong, but they do not really wait for an answer. Socialising has become far less enjoyable, as I do not speak very clearly anymore and have lost a lot of agility. I do not drive anymore, and buses are not really an option for me, as my body can stiffen without warning, making it extremely hard for me to walk. If someone picks me up and takes me out, it could work out well, or turn into a disaster. Any sign of anger, impatience or disagreement in another person can cause my body to seize up, making it difficult for me to talk, walk or smile.

So, I am locked in an increasingly secluded world with the Lord. Of course, as we all know, His manifest presence can 'hide' from us from time to time. I read, listen to audiobooks, write, do a bit of housework, and attend my Monday painting group, as well as church on Sundays.

A few months ago, these restrictions depressed me so much that I began to ask the Lord about my departure from this world. I asked Him, "Could you please tell me when You are going to call me to Yourself?"

One afternoon I was sitting in the room that I love to use for prayer. I was not actually praying. I was probably just sitting, waiting for lunch whilst enjoying the rays of summer sun streaming through the window. Then, as if in a flash, I caught a vision of a coffin, draped in white cloth with a name printed in blue. As I looked carefully at the blue print, I deciphered the words "Vera Maria Hardiman." That is my full name.

I started to panic. Was the Lord saying that I did not have very long to live? At first, I decided not to tell Ben in case it frightened him.

By that evening, I thought better of it and told him. He appeared to accept it well. The next day I made preparations. I told him what music I wanted at the funeral and that I wanted to be cremated and buried under a New Dawn rose at the Lilydale Memorial Park. I wrote notes, setting out which grandchild was to inherit which piece of jewellery. And then we waited. I was not expecting to wake up the next morning. We waited and waited. Nothing. I did not come close to dying.

When I prayed about the vision with a friend a couple of weeks later, she felt that I had a choice. The choice was to embrace life or slowly drift away.

I apologised to the Lord and repented for partnering with the spirit of death, whom we sent packing.

I assured the Lord that I was happy to stay as long as He wanted. I thanked Him for my life. I embraced life once again.

As you can see, I am still here.

# Prayer

*Please show me, dearest Lord, when I am not in sync with You.*
*I commit to doing Your will.*
*All praise and honour to You, Holy One of Israel*

# 27

# Gains

My disease has actually brought me a number of advantages. Having always been a fairly quiet introvert, I now have a good excuse to avoid social events. I am no longer asked to make speeches, nor do I have to make an effort to sound intelligent. The pressure is off.

I have learnt to be happy for the success of others. There is no need for me to succeed on any level at all.

My life had become unashamedly carefree, until the Lord convicted me. At that point I deeply and sincerely repented of my escapism and unwillingness to take responsibility. I became more responsible around the house, cooking some meals, doing some spring cleaning, and so on.

Then I had the first dream. In that dream, I was on an adventure holiday. One of the activities was surfing. The waves were very rough and turbulent. I decided to take part in the adventure, despite the apparent danger. I was confident that drowning was out of the question, as I knew I was in a spiritual dimension where I did not have to breathe. In the dream, the organisers tried to talk me out of the event. I suspected they just wanted to cancel and go home early, because of their own laziness.

It took me quite a while to interpret the dream. I later remembered that I have had series of dreams where I have been on an unmade road leading into the outback.

I interpreted those to mean that I was walking with the Lord in unchartered territory. In other words, I was facing things for which there was no grid. No instruction manual!

Anyway, in all humility, I told the Lord I would accept His challenge as I have known Him to be faithful in the past. He has a track record of getting me out of sticky situations or helping me contend through tough times.

# Prayer

Thank you, Wondrous Counsellor, for your amazing love for us.
Give us courage, that we may be Your fearless ambassadors
in a strange and alien world.

# 28

# The Pizza Dream

Then I had another dream. The second dream finished with a friend and me driving to a high-rise pizza restaurant to get some pizza. The name of the restaurant was *Agha Agha*.

A high-rise pizza restaurant is a very strange concept, perhaps indicating that it was a front for something else. Naturally, when I woke up, I felt it must have just been a pizza dream (a pizza dream is a dream you might have after a spicy meal, like pizza). The only problem was that I had not touched any spicy food, let alone pizza.

By the way, I believe "Agha Agha" is a Muslim term for a type of leader.

Earlier in the dream, I had been in a place that was literally 'godforsaken.' It felt as if there was no evidence of God's presence whatsoever. In the dream I was married to a young person who was opening up a restaurant. We were preparing the premises for a future opening, and we argued over every detail. We could not even agree about the installation of a basin for washing hands. My husband was an extremely angry man, filled with hate and despair, as if there was another agenda at play. This was not just about a restaurant. There was a political agenda. He was beholden to someone else. He was very distracted. There was no love at all between us. The place reminded me of Jordan and Bethlehem.

Of course, the Muslim title of "Agha" naturally points to an Islamic country.

I have had similar dreams about godless cities over the past two years. I am not sure of the meaning, except that they spur me to intercession.

# Prayer

*Dearest Lord, I pray that You anoint our minds
and hearts with the power of Your Holy Spirit,
that we may be able to decipher Your plans for us.
We just want to follow You, our risen
and precious Lord and Saviour.*

# 29

## Choose Your Own Adventure

Some of my readers might remember the 1980's when *Choose Your Own Adventure* books were in fashion.

They worked like this:

You could make decisions throughout the book. The book has various endings, depending on which decisions you make along the way. For example, the book might be about a main character, let us call him Leo.

Path A - Leo might decide to leave school at age 15, work in a shop and be 'discovered' by both a film producer and a basketball scout.

Path B - Leo stays at school until the end of year 12 and studies medicine or law.

Path A then gives Leo the option of becoming an actor or professional basketball player.

Path B gives him the choice of becoming a medical doctor or a lawyer.

That is how I see life. We can choose our own adventure. Choose how you respond to hardship - do you choose bitterness or forgiveness? There are consequences - each decision has a ramification or six, with attendant blessings or curses and so on.

I recently read part of Phillip Yancey's book on suffering called

*Where is God when it Hurts?*. He writes about Christian quadriplegic, Joni Eareckson. It was very comforting to read about her day-to-day life, from one moment to the next. It consoled me to learn that someone else is facing challenges similar to mine. She needs someone else to dress her and comb her hair.

Prior to the tragic accident that robbed her of so much, she was so full of life. A spur-of-the-moment decision took her life down a path of sorrow, pain, frustration, and humiliation.

Joni chose to respond with gratitude and resignation, after an initial reaction that at first took her down the road to suicidal thoughts. Grateful, after a while, and finding the fullness of life in her limiting circumstances, Joni found that even a life without mobility could be one that is well worth living.

When I received my diagnosis and my healing did not follow directly on its heels, I had two choices. I could either choose bitterness, drug and alcohol dependence or suicide, or I could choose to face my illness, make the most of what I still had and stare degeneration full in the face, daring it to rob me further.

I decided to be immersed in a hot bath at a church in Nunawading, Victoria in August 2023 as part of Todd Smith's ministry. The teaching behind the immersion was that the Lord promised to meet people in the water. Talking to several friends who also took the plunge, I found that the Lord was definitely keeping His word.

Soon after I came up out of the warm, comforting liquid, the Lord revealed to me two things about my inner self.

Firstly, He told me I was furious with Him for allowing me to get so sick. I had no idea I was so angry. In fact, as part of that revelation, I could see black liquid. I imagine that it represented the bile in my soul.

Secondly, the Lord showed me that I was carrying a huge amount of self-hatred which came from my mother's rejection of me. She had told me quite frequently that I was not the sort of daughter she had hoped for - I was not clean and domesticated, but a bit of a tomboy instead. And, to add to the disappointment, I looked like my father's side of the family.

My first response was to forgive the Lord for allowing the illness and for not healing me.

Then I went about forgiving my mother, and at the same time declaring that I was exactly as the Lord had intended me to be. I felt strengthened in my identity and finally learned to fully accept myself. It certainly helped me that my mother came to see me after she had died (in the company of Jesus and several angels and numerous relatives, whom I was not able to identify) and very sincerely apologised to me. This apology covered many, many things that I forgave her for.

# *Interlude*

Ask the Lord to meet you somewhere pretty, either in your imagination or in real life. Spend some time with Him in prayer, focussing on how much you love Him.

# Prayer

*Thank you, Jesus, for my ancestors and for teaching me about the blessings of family. Please show me what sinful practices my ancestors engaged in, so that I might be able to pray appropriately. I claim as my spiritual inheritance, any blessings passed down through believers in my family tree. I pray these things in the name of Jesus.*

# PART FIVE

# TOWARDS A
# THEOLOGY OF
# SUFFERING

# 30

## Healing Delayed

There is a gaping hole in our charismatic theology. In fact, it is the elephant in the room. How do we explain, evaluate, even talk about suffering, when we believe in a theology of healing. When we are taught to declare that the fullness of the Kingdom is here, or at least mostly here.

With the rise of the charismatic movement, the teaching on the value of suffering has fallen away to a large degree.

I was saved at a time when people in my church were being miraculously healed of serious conditions such as breast cancer and Multiple Chemical Sensitivity. In fact, miraculous healings were so common that it began to be standard practice to ask for healing and to totally expect to receive it.

As I described earlier, I saw my own father healed of cancer, for a period long enough to give him the opportunity to reconcile with family.

However, I felt that by then the emphasis was so much on healing that we could offer little comfort to sufferers of chronic illnesses. Except to promise them that, surely, healings would return soon – as soon as we had figured out the cause of their demise.

Years went by and the healings were sporadic. By the time 2021 came around, we saw very few miraculous healings in Victoria. Was it the level of sin in our State that was to blame? Could people travel elsewhere for healing? Some did and they were healed. Some found healing in the USA.

The problem was that no one wanted to admit that healings of the miraculous kind were becoming unlikely. People felt that making those kinds of statements would simply curse the situation and make everything worse for everyone.

Let me explain what I have gone through, facing illness in this age of the church. The following are my authentic perceptions and thoughts. They are my true confessions about healing in 2023.

Since my diagnosis in 2015, my experience was that I felt obliged to seek healing. It was taught from the pulpit that healing was available, we just needed to grab onto it, and it would be ours. There were no exceptions and no exclusions.

Receiving constant prayer without any dramatic shift for the better, made me feel increasingly that I was somehow to blame for this 'glitch in the system'. That my healing should have arrived but had not for some unknown reason.

I expected to be healed less and less. I had so much prayer that was only mildly effective that I lost confidence in the Lord's willingness to heal me. I definitely knew that He could heal me as I had seen it happen to other people. Yet it eluded me for some reason.

I sensed there was little faith in those who prayed for healing from Parkinson's, as there had been so few successful healings.

I felt increasingly guilty that maybe my lack of faith was preventing me from being healed. My faith certainly diminished with every unsuccessful prayer session.

This was truly a case of "hope delayed makes the heart sick." My hope in my own healing was being deferred. This very thing was making my 'heart sick.'

I read many books on the topic of healing in the hope that healing might still be possible. It must be that I had simply not learned the best way to pray in my circumstances.

I wished I could have given up on asking for healing and instead asked for prayer to accept my disease and the needed strength to endure. However, the message from my fellow believers was that it was somehow heretical to pray to be given the endurance and strength to accept my disease, to accept there would be degeneration in my brain and body.

There was little teaching and there were no appropriate books to help someone deal with a chronic illness.

If I gave up and accepted the illness, I would be more of an outsider in the church than I already was.

Writing a book on suffering and living with a chronic illness ten years after the diagnosis, makes me seem very foolish indeed.

Many people, including myself, could have benefitted from a clear theology of suffering over the past decade.

There is no doubt that there is a special grace for healing in evangelistic meetings. Yet, many healing evangelists have not been healed themselves. People like John Wimber and John Mellor went home to be with the Lord at a fairly young age. They are with the Lord now and completely healed.

My perception is that we do not want to admit to ourselves that the miraculous is not happening as frequently, so we continue to press in and press in further, demanding our miracle like the lady in the parable who hassles the judge.

It seems that whether or not one is healed can depend on where one lives and when.

There is no doubt that more healings occurred in Victoria in the 1980's than they do now. Some healing ministries do not come to my State at all, because the Lord does not release them to come. This is something not openly talked about in churches, from my experience.

There is no doubt more miracles seem to happen in poorer countries. In Kenya, for instance, I am told that many people have been raised from the dead. The level of faith in people is sometimes much higher in those places where they have to deal with totally inadequate facilities.

A friend of mine from Kenya has said that, interestingly, those who have been raised from the dead generally have a particular type of limp, which distinguishes them from other people. They will forever attest to the kindness, mercy, power and glory of the Lord in their bodies.

I believe that being healed of Parkinson's would be a miracle. The brain of a Parkinson's sufferer has nerve cells in the part of the brain called the 'basal ganglia' which have become defective or die. This leads to a reduction of dopamine being produced in the brain. Less dopamine equates to less movement and impaired fine motor coordination. The brain and the body have serious communication issues.

Only a handful of days before I began writing this chapter, the Lord gave me a revelation:

He seemed to be saying: "My people feel they are entitled to miracles. In fact, they insist on them. They forget that a miracle by its very nature is an exception to the rule, an overriding of nature. It is an exceptional thing, a wonderful privilege, a freak of nature."

It was a sobering thought.

I felt for a long time that I was entitled to be healed. The many people who have prayed with me have certainly agreed. Miracles seem to be predominantly experienced in an evangelistic setting to demonstrate the power of God and to demonstrate the future Kingdom of God breaking into the present.

A miracle by its very definition would be an exception, rather than the rule. During revivals we tend to see a lot of miracles.

I felt the Lord very lovingly straighten out my thinking and point out that we charismatics tend to act like entitled, spoiled children from time to time, insisting on our healing miracle.

No one in the history of the church has felt more entitled to be blessed. We consider ourselves to be better than past Christians, as if we were the only 'enlightened' ones. I can feel the Lord's distaste as I am writing. He opposes the proud, after all.

I believe that the Lord has revealed to me that He heals us, after which comes a time of testing. Just like the saying: "God comforts the afflicted and He afflicts the comfortable."

Whenever we have received a major healing, we find that a time of testing follows.

Being self-centred by nature, I was looking forward to being healed and being productive. I wanted so much to actually be the joyful, out-going girl that God originally designed.

I did become that girl for a brief moment in January 2009. I remember going to the funeral of a good friend's mother. I had finally overcome my social phobia and easily mixed with all the other guests.

A couple of weeks later, my brother and sister-in-law tragically died on Black Saturday, and I was again reduced to a blithering mess.

Six years later came my Parkinson's diagnosis.

The Lord pointed out to me that in this world we are being trained up to be useful in the next. That is actually a very comforting thought.

Suffering has a noble purpose - purification and training.

# Interlude

Take 20 minutes.

Ask the Lord to dictate a letter to you and write it down. Whenever I have done this activation, I have been most pleasantly surprised by His infinite goodness. I pray that you will also find this to be an extraordinary blessing.

# Prayer

*Dear Lord, I am so sorry that I have taken You for granted. Give me a healthy awe of You. I truly need to be reminded of Your vast majesty and tremendous power and holiness. I stand in awe of You, Jesus.*

# 31

## I No Longer Live

In Galatians 2:20, Paul reminds us that we have been crucified with Christ.

What does it mean to take up our cross daily? How should we live?

Paul encourages us to prefer others to ourselves. We put others first and not insist on our rights.

Elisabeth Elliott wrote about the killing of her missionary husband. He was slaughtered by the very people he was trying to reach. Then revival sprang up as a result of his death. Jim's famous words were, "He is no fool who gives what he cannot keep, to gain what he cannot lose."

When she was asked about Jim's death, Elisabeth answered that he had 'died' a long time ago. What she meant was that he had died when he gave his life to his Lord and Saviour.

Dealing with the loneliness of becoming a widow, she writes about how she had to rely on the Lord to ease the loneliness and He surely did so. She warned people against running from the pain. The secret to being comforted is to take our pain directly to the Lord, instead of seeking solace elsewhere.

I know I need to spend more time in the secret place with my dear Lord.

The Lord cheered me up one morning when He made it very clear to me that my suffering is not my fault. That knowledge brought tremendous relief to me. I had not realised how much guilt I was carrying. I was blind to the fact that I had held myself responsible for contracting Parkinson's.

Jesus also reassured people, who were blaming themselves for their sicknesses. In Chapter 9 of John's Gospel, He explains to the disciples and the blind man that he was not sick because of either his own sin or the sin of his parents.

He even explains that the suffering was there to bring great glory to God through the healing that took place.

In Luke 13, Jesus makes the same point, that illness is not always the result of sin. Just look at the following passage:

**About this time Jesus was informed that Pilate had murdered some people from Galilee while they were offering sacrifices at the Temple.**

**"Do you think those Galileans were worse sinners than the other people from Galilee?" Jesus asked.**

**"Is that why they suffered? Not at all!"**

Then He talks about those who died when the Tower of Siloam collapsed, and asks the disciples, **"And what about the eighteen people who died when the Tower of Siloam fell on them. Were they the worst sinners in Jerusalem? No."** (NLT)

There are many references to suffering in both the Old and the New Testament. In the Old Testament there are many Scriptures that emphasise that suffering is the result of disobedience to God. The cause and effect are quite straight forward. Jesus came to add further layers to our understanding of suffering.

Looking at His Word, it seems that sin will definitely cause suffering. However, the corollary is not true. Sinlessness does not protect you from suffering. Jesus is the prime example of this, along with the disciples, most of whom were brutally murdered.

To add further layers to this theology, we have the Book of Job. Job was a man who suffers unspeakably through no fault of his own. He is a faithful follower of the Lord.

His friends do not empathise. They point out that there must be hidden sin in his life.

However, as the Lord points out, there is no hidden sin in Job's life.

Could it be that the Book of Job provides shards of insight into situations like mine, where there is no obvious cause for the suffering and no prospect of healing?

Could it be true, that as with Job, suffering comes to some of us as a test. There is no point querying the Lord about this. His ways are vastly different to ours and we do not stand a chance attempting to analyse His motives. Our responsibility, when faced with this situation, is to respond to our suffering in a godly manner. We can then look forward to the purifying and edifying work suffering produces in us. Our reward will come later.

I started off looking for examples of suffering in the Bible. It was then that I realised that it was the miracles that were rare; the suffering was universal. The miracles received special attention - the Exodus, the raising of dead people, the healing at the Gate Beautiful, the raising of Lazarus.

Miraculous healing is highlighted in the Bible. It is the catalyst for extraordinary joy and amazement.

# Interlude

Ask the Lord to highlight someone
who needs an email, SMS, or phone call today.
Ask Him what and when to write to encourage that person.

# Prayer

*Lord, I do love the fact that You are with us as we weep. You deliver us.*
*You stand by us. You are our Redeemer.*
*We exalt you. O Lord.*

# 32

## The Benefits Of The Godly Response

The Bible contains examples of people's suffering being of value. There are examples of suffering people being brought to repentance, like the exiled Jews in Babylon.

The Bible teaches that patience and endurance can be the fruit of suffering, if we respond with forgiveness, patience, and a strong reliance on the Lord.

Recently, in the wee small hours, I asked Him to please explain how we are sharing in Christ's sufferings.

In response, He highlighted this scripture in Isaiah 63:9 once again. I nearly floated with joy out of bed! He gives us joy *in the midst* of our sorrow. That is part of overcoming the world.

We share in the benefit of Christ's sufferings, as we are healed, rescued, and released by His stripes.

**"In all their distress he too was distressed, And the angel of his presence saved them. In his love and mercy he redeemed them; He lifted them up and carried them all the days of old,"** Isaiah 63:9 (NIV)

Just as Jesus was incarnated to share in the life of people, we are, in our sufferings, sharing both the pain that Jesus felt as well as the pain of our fellow humans.

One concrete example of this is the fact that Lyn and I both minister in our painting group to people with brain injuries and intellectual disabilities of various sorts. By way of some glorious plan of our Saviour, both Lyn and I suffer from various disabilities connected to our defective brains. This fact, in turn, gives us an extra dose of compassion and understanding for our charges and they too, relate better to us. It is a level of incarnation which is sublimely beautiful and lovingly engineered by our Lord.

There is no doubt that many believing people suffer immensely.

St Therese of Lisieux, who is one of my role models, lived in the second half of the nineteenth century. She was a French nun who died from Tuberculosis in her early twenties, Therese, also known as "The Little Flower," was admired for the patient way she endured suffering. She writes in her autobiography, *Story of a Soul*, of the close sense of Jesus' presence she had most of her life, ever since early childhood. She was chafing at the bit to join her biological sisters and become a Carmelite nun at the earliest age possible. Intimacy with Jesus was her life's focus.

She fell gravely ill and lost her ability to sense the Lord's close presence. Ironically, when she suffered the most pain, in the last months of her life, she felt most remote from her blessed Redeemer.

She had to believe, in faith, that His presence was with her all the time.

Her story was an encouragement to me. There have been many times when there has been so much pain and discomfort in my body that I simply had to take it on trust that He was still there.

I have just had a light bulb moment.

Having given our lives to the Lord, we have completely surrendered to Him. He may do with us whatever He wills. He may allow suffering and persecution. As soldiers, we give up everything for the 'cause'.

I am not saying that the Lord inflicts suffering on us Himself. In the Book of Job, it is Satan who inflicts the suffering. God gives permission for this to happen. However, we are totally His. If that includes suffering, then so be it, as Job so rightly says.

We are followers of Jesus. Jesus suffered. We should not be surprised if we do too.

There may be a mysterious reason some followers of Jesus get sick, suffer, and are not healed. We may not understand it this side of eternity.

It is a matter of trust.

# Prayer

*Lord, there is so much of life that I do not understand. Help me to remember that indeed You are the One who has laid down Your life - "who has a claim against me that I must pay?" Job 41:11 (NIV)*

**He prunes the branches that do bear fruit, so they will produce even more.**
John 15:2 (NLT)

# 33

## Trust Him

Just as I am writing, Hamas has badly attacked Israel. They have slaughtered at least 260 young people who attended a music festival in the desert. The terrorists walked into a police station and gunned down police. They walked into private homes on kibbutzim and slaughtered families, kidnapping some people. It is a very traumatic situation at the moment.

Like many others, I have a grief heavy in my stomach. I feel grief for the innocent victims and their families. Not only soldiers, but also children and elderly women have been targeted. It is quite sickening.

When you start to think about it, there is suffering everywhere all the time. Children are being bullied in playgrounds. People are excluded and harassed at work. Car accidents cause physical and emotional pain. Congregants are not listened to at church.

Why then is suffering not discussed? Is it because people are afraid of suffering?

That is highly likely the reason. People irrationally believe that somehow suffering is contagious, so they try to distance themselves from it.

They hope that they can delay any onset of suffering by ignoring it.

For example, say the theory is indeed true that a popular weedkiller does indeed cause Parkinson's disease. I have never met anyone willing to forgo the convenience of killing weeds because there is a danger that someone nearby may contract a disease. This attitude is disgusting, but absolutely true.

Even the things God asks us to do can cause pain. Leaving a church that He does not wish us to attend any more. Or going overseas to a third world country on a mission and missing our friends and familiar food.

*The Chosen*, the excellent TV series about the life of Jesus, has an episode where Big James asks Jesus why he has not been healed. He prays that others be healed, but he is not healed himself.

In a very moving scene, Jesus points out that it is not an accident that he has not been healed. In fact, he is one of a small number who can be entrusted with suffering.

It is a controversial episode.

However, it makes sense when we look at the Book of Job.

In the Book of Job, Satan challenges the Lord. He engages in a wager of sorts. He places his bet on the likelihood that Job will curse the Lord if he has to face undeserved suffering.

Job responds well overall. He makes a statement of commitment to the Lord.

In Job 13:15, Job famously pronounces, **"Though he slay me, yet will I trust Him."** (NIV)

That is the heart attitude the Lord seeks.

We all claim that we believe the Bible is true. Why would the suffering of Job not be a pattern for thousands of others throughout history?

# Interlude

What does James 1:18 say about those who have been tested? They become the "first fruits of His creation".
Job received a double blessing after passing the test.
Meditate on that and be thankful.

# Prayer

*Heavenly Father, I am stunned that You have more wonderful things in store for us than we can possibly comprehend. I sit in silence by Your side, Almighty Conqueror.*

# 34

## Character

Suffering has the potential to build character, so long as our responses are godly. Choosing bitterness simply means that our health will deteriorate further.

**God blesses those who patiently endure testing and temptation.**
**A reward they will receive. A crown of Life as He promised.**
**We, out of all creation, became His prize possession.**
James 1:12 and 18 (NLT)

What do you see as the benefits of suffering?

I would start with a caveat. There are no benefits to be gained from suffering if you have the wrong heart attitude or response to the suffering you are facing.

The passage from James encourages me hugely. Jesus does not forget us, nor does He ignore us like the world sometimes appears to ignore those who are inconveniently ill. He is asking us to be patient and to love Him. He is ready to recognise us as His own special people.

The word that is translated as "special people" in James 1:18, is the word "aparche", meaning first fruits. The people in Revelation 14:4

(the 144,000) were also called "aparche", "the first fruits", These people refused to "play the harlot". They followed the Lamb wherever He went. Be encouraged! The Lord holds the first fruits in exceedingly high esteem.

Let that scripture sink into your soul. Appropriate it. Read it aloud over and over again.

What a wonderful God. He does not measure our usefulness to Him. He loves us always and passionately. Yet, in His kindness, He finds things for us to do. Maybe to intercede, have a meaningful conversation with someone, lay our hand on someone's hand or cheek, or "caring for orphans and widows in their distress" (James 1:27). Whatever is needed and helpful.

# Prayer

*King of Kings and Lord of Lords. You have so much compassion on us all.
I sit in silence by Your side, stunned by the wonder of You.*

# 35

## The Power Of Humility

You will have heard of the scripture:

**God opposes the proud and gives grace to the humble.** James 4:6 (NLT)

The meaning of 'opposes' is that the Lord actually stands against you. A better explanation is that by being proud, valuing our reputation far more highly than obedience to our Heavenly King, we are shutting Him out.

The word "khen", which is the Hebrew word for "grace", refers to a situation similar to a family encamped in a traditional circular encampment.

By giving us grace He is inviting us into His family, so that we come into an intimate friendship with Him. Having been given grace, we belong to the family. Accordingly, we are free to run into His tent to give Him a hug. There is freedom and security in the family camp and a beautiful sense of belonging. Apart from beauty, the word includes elements of freedom, healing, and joy.

You might be old enough to remember the old westerns we watched on TV when we were young children. These were shows like *Rawhide* with Clint Eastwood and *Wagon Train*. In both of these shows, people camped with their wagons in a circle to be safe from enemy attack.

Likewise in ancient Israel, they would camp in a circle for safety, each family having its own circle. Only family members were permitted to camp in each circle. When we receive grace, we are given entry into that secure and loving circle of wagons.[22]

If we pursue pride, on the other hand, we encounter the military opposition of God. Do we really want God to oppose us with intentionality and military force?

Or do we wish to have Him like and love us, provide us with protection, heal us, lift us up, ensure that we feel that we totally belong? It is our choice.

Sometimes suffering can lead to protection. For example, those people who were not well enough to go to work on 11 September 2001, were protected from death while they safely remained in bed when the Twin Towers collapsed.

Sometimes suffering leads to a change of direction. A Biblical example would be Joseph. He suffered greatly at the bullying hands of his brothers, but he unwittingly ended up in Egypt, where he was fêted and promoted so that, by the time there was famine in the land, he was in a unique position to provide for his family.

I also experienced a change of direction through suffering.

After my diagnosis, I eventually had to retire. That meant I was free to evangelise in the local community. This led to some enriching friendships, and I was even privileged to serve as an elder of a church for a while. That part of my life was definitely a blessing. And it brought me a sense of freedom.

As I sit here and write, I look out of the window and I see sunshine and flowers outside. I have spent this morning in my painting session at the community house. Over lunch I was unable to talk, my mouth had completely stiffened up as well as my neck. The fact that we have disabled people in the group is a real godsend. I fit in well with them. Some of them are also non-verbal. They neither judge nor pity me. I can be myself and not be concerned that they think me weird. I am so grateful that the Lord mercifully led me to that place of belonging.

# Interlude

In the Book of Revelation John writes about overcoming and the rewards of overcoming.

Read the verses below and spend some time thinking about the promises that the Lord makes to those who overcome.

In Ephesus, a promise to him who overcomes is to eat from the tree of life in God's paradise.

In Smyrna, the promise to him who overcomes is that he will not be hurt by the second death.

In Pergamum, the overcomer will be given manna from heaven and a white stone with the overcomer's new name written on it.

In Thyatira, the overcomer is promised to rule with Christ in His Kingdom.

In Sardis, the one who overcomes will be clothed in white garments and will not have his name erased from the book of life; in addition, Jesus will confess his name before the angels and the Father.

In Philadelphia, the overcomer will be a pillar in the temple of God.

In Laodicea, the one who overcomes will sit with Christ on His throne.

# Prayer

*Every so often, I have to pinch myself. I am so overwhelmed as I think*
*about Your wondrous beauty and the delights of Your character.*
*All praise to your holy name!*
*Thank you so much for the gift of life!!*

# 36

## Overwhelmed

There is an arthouse movie called *They Shoot Horses Don't They* starring Karen Black.

I am not sure if it was based on truth, but it was about a dance competition held in the depression which went on for many hours, days even.

The title suggests that sometimes people are worse off than horses. At least suffering horses get shot. People just have to keep on going.

These people were suffering so much. There was not enough to eat, but the dancers needed food to give them the energy to keep dancing. The sentiment of the movie was that animals would be mercifully shot, rather than be left to suffer as much as these people did.

The last people still dancing would win a prize. The irony was that if you had enough energy to keep dancing, you probably had enough to eat and did not really need the prize.

There have been times when I have just wanted to be home with the Lord. Even Paul felt that.

Sometimes I feel myself falling into a pit of depression. At those times I need to remind myself that the Lord is my all.

He is my comforter.

When I turn to Him, comfort comes. I have to remember to trust

Him and not to turn to chocolate or ice-cream or any other unhelpful distraction. I also need to rely on others to pray for strength and to lift me up.

We all need to remember to bring the Lord right into our emotions. Shouting at Him can be therapeutic! He can certainly take it and He loves for us to be authentic with Him. That is what intimacy is about - authentic relating.

Don't be reluctant to take anti-depressants when your health professionals recommend it. I take a medication, the side effect of which is that it elevates my mood.

Allow others to lift you up, help you out, encourage you. Share your burdens.

Surrender control. Surrender to the arms of the Lord and find an outlet for your emotions that is safe and effective.

When we all get to our place of glory, we will be incredibly happy that we endured. We will look back and see our pain as an exceedingly small price to pay.

# Prayer

*The anger and disappointment inside me make me want to explode.*
*Help me to find a way to release them.*
*Catch my heart, dearest One.*
*I trust in You. Help me to find my way back to peace.*

# 37

## The Lie About Pain

We unconsciously believe, hope and trust that life is meant to be pain free.

Which is why we are taken in by advertising that promises good feelings, comfort, and relief from pain. All we need to do is spend money and all will be well, say the advertisers.

We are duped into thinking that we are meant to do what feels good. I do not know where we picked up this fallacy. Probably during the hippie era. But it is a lie. Life is full of pain. We need to accept it, and not run away from it. Russ Harris, in his book *The Confidence Gap*, talks about socialising being a necessary thing that we do even if we find it to be painful. We are not to run away from it. It helps us with our mental health, whether we like it or not.

Even the medicines that we take and medical treatments we undergo, are not all pain-free. We need to remember that.

Once we accept that there will be pain in life, it is much easier to cope. Sometimes I just have to wait for the pain to come, and then go. This is what I was told when I lost my brother on Black Saturday. My counsellor said that if I felt no pain at his loss, then his life would have meant nothing to me. The fact that we feel grief and pain thinking about the loss of the loved ones who have passed, shows how much we care about them.

Jesus said that we are to take up our cross daily. It is not a pain free life, this Christian life. In fact, it can be exceedingly difficult. At the same time, it is filled with joy. Forewarned is forearmed; accepting that there are going to be hurdles diminishes the element of surprise. With foresight, we can better navigate the fallout that accompanies hardship and tragedy.

A tragic event can change our lives irreversibly. We need to be alert to that.

I just thank the Lord that, even with my chronic illness, I am still quite mobile after all these years. My mobility level is unstable, however. There is no way I can guarantee to be functioning well at any particular time of day, which means that I have had to reduce the number of my regular activities.

The Lord has blessed me with companions and activities that suit my condition and stimulate my creativity.

As I stated in my introduction, this book is not meant to direct you along any particular path. It is hopefully, a collection of helpful offerings. They are meant to be a source of encouragement in your time of need, whatever that may look like.

The Lord promised that He would keep our yoke easy and our burden light. Somehow this seems to contradict the warning that we will have trouble (distress, heartache, pain) in this world.

Peter, the Apostle and friend of Jesus Christ of Nazareth, warns us,

**Dear friends don't be surprised at the fiery trials you are going through, as if something strange were happening to you. Instead, be glad – for these trials make you partners with Christ in his suffering so that you will have the wonderful joy of seeing his glory when it is revealed to all the world.**
1 Peter 4: 12 (NLT)

The Lord often does not lift off our burdens, but He helps us carry them. In the meantime, He is perfecting us.

Our pride and fear are two enemies that can often get in the way. Once we learn to deal with them through repentance and prayer, the burden of suffering will lift considerably.

Again, we need to trust and accept that the Lord's ways are different from ours. We trust in His almighty goodness. We resist judging His decisions by our limited standards and within our tiny, earthly framework.

Modern day versions of Job's friends are everywhere. They are people who will ask you what you might have done to bring this suffering on yourself. I believe they are operating out of fear. They do not want to believe that this hardship could happen to them. They are doing everything in their power to prevent it through diet, exercise and more.

Let us never forget the mighty grandeur and majesty of the living God, whose ways are far, far higher than our ways.

At the conclusion of the book of Job, the Lords manifests His power and might by giving Job examples of His knowledge, wisdom, and power.

I have written out a few verses from that book in its New Living Translation.

Please join me in reading them aloud and savouring their majesty.

"Have you ever commanded the morning to appear.
And caused the dawn to rise in the east?
And made your light spread to the ends of the earth?
As the light approaches,
The earth takes shape like clay pressed beneath a seal.
It is robed in brilliant colours.
Have you explored the springs from which the seas come?
Have you visited the storehouses of the snow or seen the storehouses of hail?
Where is the path to the source of light?
Where is the home of the east wind?

Can you direct constellations through the seasons or guide the bear with her cubs across the heavens?"

Then the Lord said to Job,

"Do you still argue with the Almighty?

You are God's critic, but do you have answers?"

When confronted with His majesty, how can we presume to judge the Lord's actions or presume to develop theories concerning Him and His ways?

Let us turn our minds to our future.

What does our future hold? Let us look in Revelation 21,

I heard a loud shout from the throne saying,

"Look, God's home is now among His people! He will live with them. And they will be His people. He will wipe away every tear from their eyes. There will no longer be death or sorrow or crying or pain."

What can we possibly offer the Lord? The mighty Lord who "existed before everything was created and is supreme over all creation, for through Him God created everything in the heavenly realms and on earth."

What does the Lord ask us to do?

If I recall correctly, the prophet Micah answers with,

"To act justly, love mercy and walk humbly with your God." Micah 6:8 (NIV)

How do we do that?

As best we can under our circumstances. We must look around our own spheres of influence. How can we work towards justice and mercy for those whom the Lord has placed in our lives?

How can we be humbler as we walk with the Lord?

Never forget Jesus' words, "You are my friends if you do as I command."

We cheerfully obey out of love.

In Song of Songs, the young woman heard her lover knocking. Yet she hesitated for a moment. She had already undressed and washed her feet. For a moment she could not be bothered. Consequently, her lover left.[23] When she went looking for Him, she was beaten and bruised by the nightwatchmen. This is a mysterious passage. The outcome for the young lady appears to be quite harsh.

Let's be honest, if her heart had been completely devoted to her lover, she would not have hesitated for even a split second.

Jesus commands that we love God, and we love each other selflessly, ready to die for one another; the bar is set quite high.

In other words, we need to cry out to the Holy Spirit for the capacity to be wholeheartedly devoted to the Lord. To do what He commands and develop that ability to love unselfishly.

# Interlude

Ask yourself, "What does my Heavenly Father
wish that I do for him today?"

Sit quietly with pen and paper and write down what you hear.

# Prayer

*Thank you, Lord, that You, the Creator of the Universe, call me Your friend.*
*I would love to do something for You today, precious Lord Jesus.*
*Let me know what is on Your heart and mind today.*

# 38

## Care Packages

Prayer
*I sincerely pray that each one of my readers receive a fresh vision of the Lord through their suffering. I also pray that Holy Spirit, You comfort each one right now and ease their pain.*

Once he had repented of his pride, Job experienced a fresh vision of the Lord as well as increased blessings. Could the Lord be saying that we too, will be mightily blessed by the Lord, if we successfully make it through our trial?

The Book of Revelation makes mention of many rewards for those who "overcome". Is this a clue? Do these rewards apply to all who bear their suffering in alignment with the Kingdom of God?

There are certainly many indications in Revelation that we will be rewarded according to our deeds. Many questions remain.

In our family, whenever we have meals with extended family, we like to send people home with a so-called 'care package'. It would consist of delicious food items that were left over after the feast. And we always over cater.

Below is a care package for my readers, of thoughts I would like you to take home and contemplate.

### Holy Spirit

Always remember that Holy Spirit was sent to be our supreme comforter. Remember to ask for His assistance and infilling. He is easily grieved, so we must watch our behaviour and attitudes.

Holy Spirit was grieved, I believe, in Nazareth in Jesus' day, because the locals rejected Jesus. As a result, He was unable to perform miracles there. He could do a few healings, but miracles are obviously in a separate category.

### Miracles

I do not want to rob anyone who is meant to receive a miracle.

They are mostly evident in evangelism and when the Holy Spirit is being poured out during a revival or awakening. However, we are always encouraged to seek healing and the relief of symptoms.

### The Healthy Fear of God

We need to ask the Lord for a fresh revelation of His majesty. We need to be filled with wonder as we meditate on Yeshua the Mighty King.

### Testing

The question of testing, as in the story of Job, may be still relevant today.

Although healings are wonderful and we know that the Lord does heal, we cannot ignore the likelihood that we are being tested with suffering. The Lord does not cause it, but He does sometimes allow it. This is what happened to Job. When we are finally, fully in the Lord's presence, our suffering will seem like nothing, and we will wonder why we allowed it to unsettle us so much.

The Lord explains in the Book of Job, that there is much about our world that we will never fully comprehend. Suffering is certainly numbered amongst those mysterious things. Revelation 14:13 says "our deeds will go with us". I believe God is saying that our endurance through suffering will be greatly appreciated and acknowledged in the New Jerusalem.

### We Belong to the Lord

When we give our lives to the Lord, we give Him permission to do with us whatever He pleases. So, having given our lives to the Lord, we surrender control over to Him. If He chooses not to remove our suffering, He must have a purpose for it.

### A Limit to our Suffering

The Lord will never have us suffer beyond our capacity to endure. He is always with us, encouraging us, humouring, and strengthening us.

### Fear and Suffering

As the most dangerous part of suffering is the fear of an unknown future, we have to keep our thoughts captive and ask for the mind of Christ.

### Blame

It is important that we do not accept blame and guilt for our suffering.

We need to be able to distinguish between the nebulous, confused accusations of the enemy, and the conviction of Holy Spirit.

### Our Source of Comfort

In our sufferings I recommend that we go straight to the Lord for comfort and not seek solace elsewhere. Holy Spirit is always close by, ready to help. Alcohol and food may be tempting options, but they are unhelpful. Jesus will provide us with great comfort.

In fact, the Lord will provide solace in the most amazing, humorous, and effective ways.

### Humility

We need to embrace humility and turn our backs on pride. The

Lord promises grace to the humble. The definition of grace includes belonging, comfort, strength, healing, and more.

As always, the Lord fills us with expectation and wonder. Suffering is part of life. The Lord has forewarned us.

He is with us always. At times He carries us. There is indeed suffering that seems to be the fault of no one. The Lord has not given us an explanation of why that is the case.

We can rest assured, however, that when we are eventually with the Lord in the New Jerusalem, there will be no more pain. There will be no more grief.

In fact, the Lord promises:

**What no eye has seen, "what no ear has heard, and what no human mind has conceived" — These are the things God has prepared for those who love him And are called in accordance with His purpose.**
1 Corinthians 2:9 (NIV)

We look forward to that day!!

The Lord pokes fun at Job's self-assuredness in chapter 38 of the Book of Job:
**Where does light come from?**
**And where does darkness go?**
**Can you take each to its home?**
**But of course, you know all this.**
**For you were born before it was all created**
**You are so very experienced!**
Job 38:19-21 (NLT)

God spends some time putting Job back in his place.
Who does Job think he is?

Who do we think we are? Do we really believe that we can figure God out?

In my prayer time a few mornings ago, Jesus whispered to me that I had been 'ignoring' Holy Spirit.

He showed me that, when I pray directly to Holy Spirit, asking Him to take the pain and stiffness away from me, pain eventually leaves, and my body loosens up.

Previously, I was trying to follow the current teaching, which is to command healing in Jesus' name. Unfortunately, that does not work for me when I am feeling very vulnerable. Most of the time when I have difficulty moving and speaking, I feel weak and fragile.

This turning point has eased some of my discomfort and I am incredibly grateful.

I am learning to call on Holy Spirit's inimitable power. It seems foolish that I have not prayed this way before. I believed that I had exhausted the diverse ways of praying.

Now I must make sure that I am not being prideful in my humility! (that remark was intended to bring a smile to your face).

There actually is a way to pray that brings some relief to my suffering. Like Job, I am left quite speechless at this turn of events and, like Job, I have to stay teachable.

# Prayer

*We join all those gathered in Heaven's throne room and declare
that all praise be to the Lamb that was slaughtered.
To You be all honour, glory, power, wisdom, and strength,
forever and ever.
Amen.*

*Oh, glorious Trinity, thank You for Your fresh revelation.
Keep us all teachable and dependent on You, day by day.*

# 39

## The Blood Of Jesus

In a few days it will be exactly nine years since I was diagnosed.

I am sitting up writing at 5am on a Monday morning, The Lord spent two hours with me over the weekend, pointing out all the things I feel guilty about in my life. I felt ashamed of the way I had failed my parents, my husband, my children, my fellow Christians, and my dear friends. The many horrid things I have done and the many loving things that I ought to have done but failed to do.

The Lord brought them all back to my remembrance in the early hours of this morning.

I had a profound sense that I have been punishing myself severely for the past nine years.

The wonderful truth finally sank into my heart that Jesus has already died for me by shedding His blood on a nasty first century execution device to the point of death. So that I did not need to bear that punishment.

I was free to go. I simply needed to accept His gift of complete exoneration.

I finally grasped the truth He has been trying to tell me for so long.

Glory to God for revealing it to me. Glory to the Slain Lamb for paying an extremely high price for me and my many shortcomings.

How great is His love for us.

A couple of days ago I had prayer with an old acquaintance I had not seen for thirty years. I felt as if I had stepped out of a grave. Life and love seeped into my being and something was restored that I had not felt for an exceedingly long time. Courage and a zest for life are returning to me.

# Prayer

*Lord, I thank you for a new infilling.*
*You are always full of surprises, Almighty Saviour and Lord.*
*You have brought me hope.*

**Worthy is the Lamb, who was slain, to receive power and wealth**
**and wisdom and strength and honour and glory and praise!**
Revelation 5:11 (NIV)

# 40

# The Sufferer's Secret Assignment

For all those suffering I bring a message of great hope.

It is most likely that you are being prepared for one of the Lord's special assignments.

You are in the refinement process. A type of intensive boot camp. A fast tracking to 'promotion' if you prefer to see it that way. Mind you, it is an upside-down Kingdom. A 'promotion' could be a greater opportunity to serve sacrificially. It is a place of character development. A purification.

As we follow His unmistakable voice we will be given brand new assignments. A secret mission perhaps. A calling to a hard and obstinate people? Or to a country in dire poverty? A call to speak to the person sitting next to you on the bus? A call to intercession?

Take a look at the lives of so many Biblical characters - Abraham, Joseph, Moses, and King David are well known examples of this. They had to suffer and grow before they entered into their destinies. Some for many years.

The Lord gave me an interpretation of my pizza dream. After a little bit of prayer and contemplation, it dawned on me that it was set in Gaza. It was a call to pray for Gaza.

Also, in my prayer time, I felt a prompting from the Lord. There is something new on the horizon for me, I am not quite sure what it will be. The very thought of it excites my spirit. It is always a privilege to partner with Holy Spirit to bring honour to our wonderful Saviour.

Don't be discouraged by your particular circumstances. You may be in great pain. You may be immobile and even non-verbal. The power of intercession, even without words, can be fierce and extremely effective. The Lord has an assignment for you.

There is no doubt about that.


**Surprise Healing**

Last Sunday morning, the Lord surprised and challenged me again.

To put things into context, I have had a lot of trouble breathing lately, which in turn meant that I wasn't sleeping well.

At about 2.30am on Sunday, 7 July, 2024, I was lying awake and had a vision, or daydream, that I was in heaven receiving prayer from a team from the 'cloud of witnesses'. I was vomiting in the daydream. The team was led by none other than Miriam, as Jesus' mother is known in Hebrew.

It was as if I had vomited out whatever had been hindering my breathing. Suddenly, my breathing passages cleared dramatically and since then I have been sleeping very soundly each night.

I am ecstatic about this development!

Doesn't God love to challenge our theology? I have a sneaking suspicion that the Lord wants the denominations to stop judging and demonising each other. This applies especially to Catholics and Protestants. How confronting, especially for my Protestant readers, that the Lord would involve Mary in a healing!

There is no doubt that we Protestants have undervalued Mary, who is, according to Luke, the most blessed of women. John, in chapter 12 of Revelation, calls her the mother of all who obey God.

Like Mary, we are left with much to ponder in our hearts.

# Prayer

*Lord, I am so grateful that You allow us the privilege of partnering with You in Your amazing work. Thank you, Lord, that the Christian life is such a marvellous adventure. All glory to You, Mighty Yeshua.*

*I pray for my readers, that they will endure well and finish well. Fill them with Your glorious hope, blessed Redeemer. Strengthen them. Give them powerful, divine encounters to encourage them. Kindly grant them a manifest experience of Your unfathomable love. All praise to You, O Glorious One! King of All, the worthy Slain Lamb.*
*May the Lord bless you mightily, dear reader.*

**'May the Lord bless you**
**and protect you.**
**May the Lord smile on you**
**and be gracious to you.**
**May the Lord show you his favour**
**and give you his peace.'**
Numbers 6:24-26 (NLT)

*Vera Hardiman is a retired lawyer living on the outskirts of Melbourne, Australia with her husband, Ben, family dog, Alex and two very needy cats. Vera spends her time volunteering and dabbling in creative pursuits like painting and writing.*

# References

1.  Acronyms: NLT New Living Translation; NIV New International Version

2.  An evangelistic course based on a study of the Gospel of Mark

3.  levodopa /carbidopa

4.  Fast acting levodopa/carbidopa

5.  Person with Parkinson's

6.  John 15: 14

7.  Genesis 1

8.  Black Saturday was a day of immense destruction. Firestorms killed 173 people and completely destroyed a number of towns in Victoria, Australia. It occurred during a summer of very high temperatures and extremely dry conditions.

9.  Australian healing evangelist.

10. Dystonia

11. John 14:28

12. John 16:15

13. William Shakespeare, Sonnet 43

14. Psalm 34:18 NIV

15. Isaiah 49:16 NIV

16. Matthew 28:20

17. Marmorkuchen literally translates as "marble cake". It is usually both chocolate and vanilla. When you cut it, there are dark brown and pale swirls, resembling marble.

18. Revelation 21:4

19. Rick Renner, Greek I p. 792

20. Joel 2:25

21. Romans 8:23 (NLT)

22. The humble receive grace. "Grace" means I live in the favour of God. He smiles on me and showers me with benefits of all kinds. Both the Greek and Hebrew word for "grace" "charis" and "khen" point to a wide range of amazing benefits. One translation of charis is: the powerful presence of God which is capable of ensuring any kind of restoration and redemption.

The Hebrew word ("khen") for "grace" also points to "belonging", In other words, the right to camp in the circle of the family, where there is healing, protection, encouragement, belonging, strengthening, being a part of God's family.

23.    Song of Songs 5: 2 -7

# Bibliography

Russ Harris, The Confidence Gap (Melbourne, 2010: Penguin Books)

Philip Yancey, where is God When it Hurts? (Grand Rapids MI USA: Zondervan Press 1977)

Eric Metaxas, Dietrich Bonhoeffer Pastor, Martyr, Prophet, Spy (Nashville, Tennessee 2010: Thomas Nelson)

Therese Lisieux, Story of a Soul, (Washington DC USA 1996:ICS Publications)

Elisabeth Elliott, Omnibus: Through the Gates of Splendour, Shadow of the Almighty, No Graven Image (Carlisle, UK 1997)

Rick Renner, Sparkling Gems from the Greek Volume 1 (Shippensburg, 2003)

Rick Renner, Sparkling Gems from the Greek Volume 2 (Shippensburg, 2016)

# Reference Books

The Strong's Expanded Exhaustive Concordance of the Bible (Nashville, TN USA 2010: Thomas Nelson Publishers)

Interlinear Bible (USA 2011: Hendrickson Publishers) s

Jeff A. Benner, Ancient Hebrew Lexicon of the Bible (College Station TX USA 2005:Bookworm.com)

Printed in the USA
CPSIA information can be obtained
at www.ICGtesting.com
LVHW071450110924
790749LV00016B/218